THE GAME THE GOAL

THE
GRANT FOX
STORY

THE GAME THE GOAL

THE GRANT FOX STORY

with Alex Veysey

rugby press limited
Auckland

*The author and publishers wish to thank all those
photographers and organisations who have contributed
to this book, notably Peter Bush of Wellington, Andrew
Cornaga and Kenji Ito of Auckland.*

© 1992 Rugby Press Ltd
First published in 1992 by Rugby Press Ltd
67-73 View Road, Glenfield, Auckland 10, New Zealand.

Layout/design by Sportz Graphics Ltd, Glenfield, Auckland.
Typeset by Sportz Graphics Ltd.
Cover art by Grant Hanna, Auckland.
Printed by Colorcraft Ltd, Hong Kong.

Rugby Press Ltd is a member of the Medialine Group
of companies. P.O. Box 100-243, North Shore Mail Centre,
Auckland 10. New Zealand.

ISBN 0-908630-39-5

To ERIC Best Wishes
Tony

Xmas '97

Contents

To my family support group. . .Adele, Ryan and Kendall
– one day soon I'll give back all that time; Pam and Ian,
who can drive the Te Puke-Auckland road in their sleep;
Merv and Yvonne, always there when I'm away.

Foreword

"Give it to me. I'll take it." I well remember the day in 1982. Wet, windy, ground greasy. Auckland playing Manawatu at Eden Park. Only minutes to go in the game and Auckland are behind by a point or two. If we lose this one, we can kiss goodbye to any hope of taking out the National Championship. We've never won it. Penalty awarded 40 metres out. I've kicked a few big ones in my time. I'll take it. It's really our last chance. I move forward and grab the ball. Alwyn Harvey, the skipper, looks over, uncertainty written on his face. That's when the young fella speaks. "Give it to me. I'll take it."

Snowy, curly hair. Fresh faced, slightly built. Nineteen years old in his first year of representative rugby. I'm immediately struck by the confidence in his voice. I ponder briefly and then hand over the ball. I retreat to my position at fullback and watch...the precise digging of the hole and placing of the ball. The measured walk back and two steps to the left. The deep breaths...the shaking of the fingers. Here he goes...even, rhythmical, the swing of the leg, thump! It looks on line. Is it long enough? Wait! The flags are up. You bloody beauty Foxy. You've done it! You ripper.

How often have we seen it since. Grant Fox, master goalkicker, master tactician, maker of tries, matchwinner. The greatest point scorer in New Zealand rugby history and he's still playing. Most capped All Black first five-eighths. The records will surely continue to fall.

As we've all watched this maestro perform so expertly these past ten seasons or so, it has been easy to assume that his skills and abilities have come naturally. This view, however, belies the enormous number of hours of practice that has honed the legend's skills. I have been associated with Grant Fox from the beginning of his first-class career as a team-mate and latterly as back coach of the immensely successful Auckland team of the 1980s. I have never ceased to be amazed at the man's dedication and diligence. Consistently early to training, he practises his whole range of skills. Goalkicks, dropkicks, line kicks both left and right foot, bombs, plenty of time receiving passes from his halfback of the day and moving it wide with lovely spiral passes off both hands. The day before the match he is down to the playing venue for at least an hour's kicking, testing the vagaries of the wind. The ritual has never ceased.

Surely, now that he's recognised as one of the all-time greats, one would think the dedication might wane. Not on your nelly. And this, perhaps, tells the story of this oft misunderstood man. Intensely proud, loyal, serious, moody, restless, Foxy is a perfectionist. He wants it to be perfect for himself and he wants it to be perfect for the team. He's willing to go the extra mile, to put in the hard yakka. And he expects his team-mates to do the same. He doesn't suffer fools gladly but rugby at the top level is not a fool's game. He's the winningest player I have seen and his team-mates are thankful for it. Both John Kirwan and Terry Wright, the two wing threequarters whose first-class careers have almost parallelled Fox's, are among the most prolific try-scorers in New Zealand rugby history at first-class level and they have each scored prolifically in test rugby. Thanks Foxy.

His contribution to Auckland rugby this past ten seasons has been immeasurable. Analytical, thoughtful and never afraid to speak his mind, he has been a major contributor to the tactics and the methods of this great team. His intense determination, his desire to succeed and his fear of failure have permeated the team. I have been asked many times what has made the Auckland team of this era so good. We've had some great players. But a powerful component has been the spirit and the striving for excellence which Grant Fox has imbued in the side. And while I have not been involved with the All Blacks in the 1980s or the 1990s, I know that the same applied to them as well. History has shown us that most great teams do not hold their peak for more than three years. Grant Fox's Auckland and All Black teams have stretched that statistic to an extent which may never be equalled.

Grant Fox is a once-in-a-lifetime player and team man. A winner.

Bryan Williams
April, 1992

Introduction

Grant James Fox is an All Black this year first because he
loves to play rugby and second because he refused, following the All Blacks' defeat in the World Cup of 1991, to back
out of the game in humiliation while under serious public
criticism for his World Cup performance. So he set himself up to
be dropped rather than retreat from that challenge, played in the
trials before the New Zealand Rugby Football Union centennial
matches and came through as a first five-eighths and goal-kicker
the selectors wanted. Significantly, this was a new panel of
selectors. Fox was under scrutiny from three men who owed no
allegiance to any act of the previous panel and whose selections
even at trials level vigorously underlined their independence.
They were seeking to change the tactical formula because it had
become clear the old one had been picked to the bones by those
who had had to counter it through its most glorious years and
who, while now on top of it, sought to preserve its tastiest
morsels to stitch in to their own strategies.

That was the greatest compliment to a team the Australian
captain, Nick Farr-Jones, in his foreword to photographer Peter
Bush's book *Pride, Power and Pain*, said was, arguably, the greatest
rugby team in the history of the game. "As long as rugby is played
and talked about the 1987-91 All Black era will dominate
conversation and memories."

The nature of such a tribute from one of the great players of
rugby calls into question the treatment by many New Zealand
rugby followers of some of the men who created that era, Fox
being notable among them, when finally the Australians under
Farr-Jones ended it on the other side of the world on Lansdowne
Road, where the turf seems to be greener and lusher than

anywhere else that rugby is played.

In the public backlash following that defeat the heroes of the great era which saw the All Blacks playing 50 matches without loss were transformed into the dregs of rugby society. They were booted about with contempt, an astonishing aberration in a country the international mana of which rests most comfortably on its achievements in sport and sportsmanship.

For much of the semi-final match against Australia, Fox played with an injury which reduced his effectiveness by 50 per cent and that is unacceptable in a match demanding 100 per cent from every player. Nor was he alone in this. He has dwelt painfully on the decision he took to stay on the field when the game was 30 minutes old. The co-coach of the team, John Hart, says, "He should have come off. But I understand why he didn't. And nor in that match in the same circumstances would I have come off."

A year before, Fox had been voted New Zealand Rugby Player of the Year, an honour he had also won in 1988. In the year between, the French named him the International Rugby Player of the Year. He is a reluctant recipient of individual honours... "Rugby is the ultimate team game. No individual can achieve without his mates." There is truth in that. But there is truth also in the statistics he eschews that in his 35 tests for New Zealand until the end of 1991 he scored 525 points, an average of 15 a game and that in that time 51 per cent of his points per game were registered in the 10-19 bracket and 26 per cent over 20. At that stage for Auckland he had scored 2281 points in 155 games. He himself would be surprised to know that in that total were 80 points from tries.

Fox dominated games in the sense that both his own team and the opposition planned for him. His kicking to goal was so accurate that he put a brake on the game-plans of opposing teams and his own team had the built-in confidence of knowing that when their pressure on their opponents encouraged penalties they had in Fox a kicker who rarely missed. The schedule of kicking practice he sets out in this book emphasises that even now he does not take his astounding ability as a kicker for granted. It is a daunting programme yet he demands it for himself in the fairest and the foulest of weather.

Fox is an intense and serious man. There is a wry strain of humour in him but in the company of other players, mostly he is the entertained rather than the entertainer. Hart recalls that when Fox came into his Auckland squad in 1982 he was "very serious, strong-willed, single-minded." For Fox it was a case of learning first to listen, then of learning. Hart says that when he first watched Fox playing for the Auckland Grammar School first XV it was easy to detect the intensity with which he pursued dominance in his tactical control of matches.

That never changed. Grizz Wyllie, his All Black coach after the World Cup of 1987 through to the World Cup of 1991, says, "He is such a determined little bugger. So committed to rugby and the team. He gives 100 per cent of himself and he demands 100 per cent from everyone else. I have wondered at times whether he is not too intense about it all. Maybe at times it has rubbed off on to others. But if everyone had his dedication what a hell of a squad a coach would have to work with." Wyllie says the concentration Fox turned to the practice of his craft was "almost bloody frightening" and the pressure he placed on himself to succeed "sometimes too much even for him to handle." And he pointed to Fox's distress when, after the All Blacks had come back from a big deficit to be 19-19 against the Australians at Brisbane in 1988, he had to convert John Kirwan's try for the win. From wide out the kick missed and Wyllie says Fox blamed himself for what was no more than "a bit of a bloody smudge" on the All Blacks' record but which he saw as some sort of personal tragedy.

It is worth the record that for all the public divisiveness over the respective qualities of Hart and Wyllie as coaches both wanted Fox as the first five-eighths. And when they were gone so did the new selectors. John Hart had a vision for Auckland rugby. To achieve it he required new discipline from the players so that he could build a different style of game. He thought it would take three years before he could expand the Auckland game to the state he envisaged for it. In his first squad was Grant Fox because, says Hart, "I recognised then he was much more than being a great reader of rugby. He had such vision for a young player. There were limitations. He couldn't run and at that stage he was a bit of a shoveller, but what a fabulous kicker. We worked together at his flexibility and as that developed he became a catalyst in Auckland's progress from vision to reality."

Fox denigrates his own running ability.... "If there's a big gap you could drive a team of oxen through I'll take it." Hart says he never became a great runner because, physically, he didn't have the wherewithal. It was in that realisation that Hart brought in fine running half-backs like Richard Dunn, Tim Burcher, David Kirk and, with good runners on the outside, he found the mix worked.

The criticism of Fox as a passer of the ball persisted but Hart points to the tries scored for Auckland by John Kirwan, Terry Wright and Lindsay Harris, running in from full-back... "Grant became a very, very complete first five-eighths. He was a master tactician, a brilliant tactical kicker of the ball and his passing game developed well. With players like Andy Haden and Joe Stanley he was fundamental to the game I wanted played."

Hart remembers the game and the try from which he took the satisfaction of knowing his vision for Auckland rugby was now a matter of fact. It was against Queensland at Brisbane in 1984... "It had been instilled in New Zealand rugby that you did not, could not, attack on the open side from scrums. But here Fox, with brilliant passing, set up one of the greatest tries I have ever seen. The ball went through eight or nine pairs of hands. It was the definitive answer to anyone who queried whether Fox could play this sort of game. It was the transition for him from tactical kicker to all-round player."

When Fox, against the judgement of more experienced players in the backline, drop-kicked the goal which gave Auckland a win over the 1983 Lions at the game's last gasp, he was saying, in effect, "This is what I am". In only his second season of representative rugby he was in control, confidently making his decision in a high-pressure situation, prepared to back himself.

Hart says it was a great tragedy for rugby that Fox was condemned after the World Cup campaign... "after all those years as a match-winner for New Zealand, that he should be so cruelly treated by New Zealanders was a stain on rugby in this country."

Fox says in his book, "I can be a little prick on the field". But he explodes the rumour that he was responsible for the Canterbury half-back, Bruce Deans, being dropped from the All Blacks in 1989 in favour of Graeme Bachop, one of a trail of rumours which made the last year or two difficult to bear, perhaps not so much for the rumours themselves but for the credence they were given. His confession that he can be overly demanding of young players is also his statement of a principle he holds dear. He is saying he is unable to accept that talented players will sit back on talent believing it to be enough when with hard work they could become great players. He is a hard-work missionary and has been since he was a youngster becoming aware that he lacked the natural physical gifts which would make him an instinctive ball player. By sweating at it for long hours he became what he is in rugby but also a good cricketer, tennis player and golfer.

An old mate of Grizz Wyllie's and just as hard a man, Fergie McCormick, himself one of the great All Blacks, said after watching Fox in one of the early 1987 World Cup matches, "When he kicks for touch he finds it. When he goes for the tackle he makes it and when he kicks for goal he puts them over. He's a real test five-eighths. He doesn't make mistakes, he's not frightened and he has a bit of guts." That coming from one such as McCormick was just about the ultimate accolade. And it is the more interesting because from time to time Fox has been criticised

Getting angry – probably at himself.

for his defence. Former All Black captain (and a courageous man on the tackle) Graham Mourie after the 1987 World Cup final: "On the rare occasions the French penetrated, Grant Fox threw himself into the fray with some courageous tackles."

As a veteran now and the holder of just about every points-scoring record devout rugby statisticians can dream up, Fox, for all his years, was still the angry young man of New Zealand rugby in 1991. Through the years his anger was directed more at himself than others but it certainly ricocheted off in many directions. His long-time team-mates found it amusing when Foxy cut loose in a game and it became a dressing-room joke in which he joined. But his demands upon himself became, also, his demands upon other, younger, players and where he sought bounce-back from them he got none. He says, "Had Craig (Innes) been able to bring himself to say, 'Gotcha, Foxy. Now shut up' or had Walter (Little) been able to say, 'You buggered that up, Foxy. Pull yourself together' I'd have died happy."

Gary Whetton said in the magazine *Sunday*, "He is such a perfectionist. He'll get angry at himself. He is very hard – too hard – on himself for such a good player. There's no need for it. Everyone respects him." It may be that Fox does not understand the deep respect in which he is held by such long campaigners as the Whettons, John Kirwan and Joe Stanley. Hart says their respect for Fox is limitless.

For all the impatience, all the built-in restlessness, Fox projects his warmth and concern in many ways. His wife, Adele, talks of his eagerness to go the extra mile if it will help or comfort the aged and the very young to whom he is still a hero. Fox himself recalls the funereal climate of the All Black dressing room after a test won against Argentina but with Michael Jones's knee appallingly damaged... "Then it all changed. This bubbly little kid, a Down's syndrome boy, came into the dressing-room and transformed it. We put Kipper's (John Gallagher's) jersey on him and he went around the room talking to all the boys. He knew all of us by name. He was in some sort of seventh heaven and he lifted us up there with him, too. He asked for the national anthem and the haka and he got both. He gave us warmth and animation when we felt down."

These are the same men some would call the unsmiling giants, the arrogant ones.

New Zealand's internationally noted rugby writer T.P. McLean wrote recently "the possibility grows stronger that, one of these days, a huge statue of Grant Fox will be put on North Head, the superb conical height at the entrance to Auckland's Waitemata Harbour. By now, the man deserves something more tangible than a place in the history books".

The French usually have a more sensitive phrase than most to fit any conditions or circumstance. It was they who, having named Grant Fox Rugby Player of the Year, said: "He has marked and will continue to mark the countenance of modern rugby." There is a message in that for all New Zealand.

Grant Fox, by Adele Fox

It has become fashionable for rugby wives to say their piece in their husbands' books. I am not interested in being part of that as a fashion.

Andy Haden's wife, Trecha Haden, was, in her way, one of rugby's true pioneer women, seeking recognition from the administration of the day that the wives and girl-friends of the players were due the social courtesies and the common respect within rugby that they had as of right outside rugby.

Things have changed from the bad old days, thanks to women like her and players who would not stand by while their wives and friends were deliberately isolated from the game's social activities while the wives of administrators were caught up in the elite whirl. Consequently, I have much for which to thank rugby. I would not have swapped the years I have had, actually being made to feel I am inside the game and having the company of other rugby families.

It is unfortunate that as those things have changed so have the demands on the players. The game has become all-powerful, requiring its players to commit themselves to an ever-increasing schedule of matches and tours, demanding their "professionalism" in all things, in time, in efficiency, in fitness – in everything except material professionalism, the real McCoy. They are demands which have placed what are at times unendurable pressures on families as they try to make do without husbands and fathers. I say that from the heart and from the hearts of our children, Ryan and Kendall.

As long as rugby players who want to be top players have to turn professional time and effort to the game while holding down their five-day-a-week jobs, families will suffer. I know of one family of an outstanding All Black of recent years which is on the breadline. Whose fault? His? Or the fault of a system which says if you want to be an All Black, suffer.

I do not speak for Grant when I say that as a multi-million dollar business rugby, to survive with its outstanding players and for its outstanding players to survive with their families, has to become professional, fully paid-

Another tour, another homecoming – to Adele and Ryan.

up professional. I know that goes against the grain of a game which is profoundly proud of its amateur traditions, as it should be. But the rules have changed and, ironically, they have changed when economically the players, as part of the whole working community, can least afford to be away from their jobs. I cannot see why countries like New Zealand and Australia, which are at least conscious that times have changed and that there is desperation out there, should be held back by such as the British who make noises about New Zealand players being professionals without knowing that, still, New Zealanders by and large are the most amateur in the world.

I wanted to have a voice, however small, in Grant's book to say some things he would not dream of saying about what he gives to rugby and what he gives to people in concern and time. I wanted to put it on the record that he and his wife and children suffer from cowardly attacks on his character by anonymous people given a voice, given credibility and given encouragement by such media outlets as talk-back radio.

Top sportsmen will always be criticised. It seems to be part of some strange plan of life that once the public has built a man into a hero it then must seek to reduce him to less than life-size by any means. Oddly, in this world of relative equality, the same does not apply to sportswomen. The fact is top sportsmen expect criticism, expect criticism which is fair and have come to expect criticism which is patently unfair and often inspired by ulterior motive. I believe the criticism which built up against individuals in 1991 was disgusting coming from people who see themselves as rugby lovers.

Such insults as were aimed at Alex Wyllie, Gary Whetton, John Hart and Grant have no part in rugby.

Our son Ryan is five. He loves to hold a ball of any shape or a bat or a racquet. I hope he plays a team sport, no matter what, because I think team sport is an important part of a child's education. But may he never have to tolerate such criticism as has come his father's way and may he never indulge in it at the expense of others. That, too, will be part of his education. He has heard comments on radio and they bewilder him. He asks, "Why do they say that about daddy? What did daddy do wrong?"

So much criticism comes from people who achieved nothing in their sporting lives. I must say I have become very defensive about it all. Things which I should be able to laugh off as mindless and cowardly hurt me. While Grant was still in Britain for the World Cup a letter was sent to him care of the New Zealand Rugby Union. It was passed on to me. It contained a newspaper clipping and scrawled around it were derogatory comments clearly designed to hurt. It was laughable, of course, that the guy who wrote it (from Taumarunui) called Grant gutless among other things but didn't have the manliness to sign his name. But I'm afraid I couldn't laugh.

I say, too, that ex-All Blacks who have had their time of glory and who have themselves reacted angrily to distant criticism should stay away from the microphones and the cameras if all they have to offer for their pay is destructive personal criticism of current players. It just seems to me that among some of these critics there is an eagerness to push themselves to the forefront, as if they cannot cope with the loss of their own fame, and that they see the best way to make a new impact is through the macho business of criticism. Measured commentary is one thing and acceptable. Simplistic destruction is another and not acceptable.

At the risk of appearing an over-protective rugby wife I rang one newspaper rugby critic following a remarkable attack on Grant and what was alleged to be his undermining influence on other players on the field. I was as much curious as angry when I asked whether the writer had actually spoken to these "other players". He admitted he had not and said that what he had written was opinion. He added something like, "Look, if he plays well next week I'll write him up as a hero." Funny that.

On the other side of the coin there are the heart-warming letters and calls from people who just want Grant to know they appreciate what he has done for New Zealand rugby. And there are the relationships Grant has built up with fans from age 6 to 100. "Dear Mr Fox, I love you. I am six. Jason."

Brett McEwan is a regular seven-year-old correspondent from Wallacetown in Southland. He wrote and told Grant he had chicken-pox, so Grant rang him and the response was so disbelieving, so spontaneous that other things which made you bitter seemed much less important.

Colin Jones was 100 when Grant first met him. The matron of the rest home where Colin was living rang and asked whether Grant could possibly visit him. He did and he went back for Colin's 101st and 102nd birthdays. He arranged with the Auckland Rugby Union to have Colin picked up in his wheelchair and taken to the official box at Eden Park to watch a Ranfurly Shield match. They became such good friends. When Grant was leaving for the World Cup, Colin sent a card telling Grant all the patients would be thinking of him. When Grant came home Colin had died.

Grant receives marvellous pastel portraits of himself from Jone Cinavilakeba, of Nasimi Village in Fiji and he replies and sends rugby posters which, evidently, make a big hit in the village.

Alan Dale, the Jim Robinson of Neighbours, is a rugby nut. They met during the World Cup and became friends. Alan wrote, "I shall remember that week for the rest of my life."

Old people from all over the place let Grant know he is appreciated and he takes the time to reply to them. There's Derrick Solomon Mulligan from

Just a couple of footy fans – with Colin Jones.

The cool technique of Foxy Junior

Player and Supporter of the Year, 1988.

Opotiki, Joe Fox and his 80-year-old mother from Otara. A Lower Hutt grandmother in her 70s wrote: "Thank you personally for the pleasure your play has given me. Your dedication and hours of practice will never be forgotten. You have never been given the credit or recognition you deserve for your great service to the game."

When the criticism of Grant was at its height he received something like 60 letters from people pleading with him not to heed it. There are so many things that are not known about him and which he would never write about himself, the things which are on the fringes of the game but which mean so much to its image. Who knows that he gives his time to help young players after his own training? That he becomes involved with children stricken with debilitating illness?

Is it not ironic that he is some sort of hero in Japan, a regular cover-boy in rugby magazines there, and that from as far away as Germany he is sought to promote the game, while here where he has done so much to contribute to the All Blacks' fabulous record, he is now subjected to such harsh criticisms, often by faceless, nameless cowards?

Having said all that, I need also to say rugby is a great game. I love watching it and always will. I feel very lucky to have been part of the wonderful Auckland and All Black era. We have been marvellously treated by an Auckland Rugby Union which has genuine sensitivity to its players' needs.

1

Barefoot in Paradise

So here I am. They're playing God Defend New Zealand and I'm standing on the greenest stretch of turf ever sown by mortal man. My right hand is across my chest clutching the silver fern and I'm singing as close to the tune as I can get, but with all the racket it's hard to tell how close that is. Probably I hit about the same proportion of bum notes as Richard Loe. Or even Sean Fitzpatrick. That means we wouldn't be giving the Mobil Song Quest much of a shake. At least the band makes the tune recognisable for the crowd. Notoriously, the All Blacks are not choristers, more your self-conscious mumblers singing along an octave below the true key. But here we have an excuse. There are other, weightier, matters on our minds. This is Dublin, Sunday, October 27, 1991. It is Lansdowne Road and the World Cup semi-final, the semi-final everyone seems to be calling the true final (except the administrative gentlemen who needed a southern hemisphere knock-out job done in Dublin). I am edgy. As always, the preliminaries are taking too long. I want to be in the game. The game: It would be a wry joke were it not so serious. Here we are, 12,000 miles across the world, but for the lush spread of the grass and the distinctive sounds of the Irish we might as well be at Ballymore Park or Concord Oval, Eden Park or Lancaster Park with the ornate bucket we call the Bledisloe Cup glittering away on the sideline. For there they are again, glaring us down, macho as hell as we get into the haka (all except Campo who is playing his own eccentric little ball game 40 metres away). The bloody Aussies.

We call them that in the nicest way, the sort of abusive affection we seem to reserve for each other. It may not always be apparent to a public which is inclined to put its own dire construction on graphic finger-type gestures and unheard words when Phil Kearns scores a try underneath Fitzy or when Peter FitzSimons and Stevie McDowell compare head-to-head or

The bum-note choirboys – before the World Cup semi-final, 1991.

stud-to-stud combat efficiency. But the fact is that beneath the crusty surface there is, even 12,000 miles from home, a brotherhood none but the players can define. It has its base in mutual respect but, without getting maudlin about it, there is in it, too, the stuff of historic comradeship.

For some of us there is a contest going back to the days when we first started feeling our rugby oats – or any sort of oats for that matter. Michael Lynagh and I go away back...when was it? When the Australian Colts knocked off the New Zealand Colts in 1982 and 1983. Lynagh and Fox, first five-eighths to first five-eighths. And out there on the wing, that flashy kid with a name straight out of a Godfather movie. Campese. And further back, in 1980, playing for Australian secondary schools against us, the first New Zealand schools team to tour overseas, at Manuka Oval in Canberra, a whole bundle of future Wallabies...Brett Papworth the brilliant young midfielder who went to league, David Knox, World Cup squad five-eighths, and in the forwards Steve Tuynman, Tom Lawton, Cameron Lillicrap and Damien Frawley. We cut them up in the backs, led 19-6, lost 13 scrums against the head, led 19-18 and conceded a penalty in the last couple of minutes to lose the game.

It was on that tour, at a time when the rules on professionalism were so suffocating that, in the clinical sense, I probably disqualified myself from rugby union for ever. We had the Wairarapa-Bush player Mark Benton at fullback and his dad came over for the tour. As a spectator at the first game at Rockhampton he backed me, kick by kick, to place the goals. He had plenty of takers. I mean, they only had to look at me for a start. They saw a skinny little scrubber with funny-shaped legs but it was one of those days when they kept going over from everywhere.

After I'd kicked 10 out of 10 Benton senior had made a bundle and not long afterward he became very, very happy. He shouted me what might have been a lemonade but for the amber colour and the froth on top. And he shouted me another. So, here I make my first confession that I have knowingly accepted payment in kind from the profits of gambling on an amateur game. I make it only in the confidence that the New Zealand Rugby Union has come a long way since 1980 and that, anyway, it now frowns upon retrospective punishment.

I am told that when I was in my first year at Auckland Grammar a master saw me kicking a ball around and said to another that "the little kid with chicken legs" seemed to have promise. He was right about the legs. He might say much the same today. They sure aren't your model athletic specimens. You could say my right leg is downright peculiar. There's a bawdy little verse about a chap with bandy legs which doesn't bear repetition here other than to note that mine, too, are like parentheses.

If you covered the rest of us and exposed my right leg alongside that of Michael Lynagh you would have one of sport's more bizarre comparisons. I suppose the miracle is that it works at all. When I was in my fourth form year I tore a hamstring in my right leg badly playing in a trial game. Something just went bang and one hammy was torn off at its attachment. The chiropractor said then the shape of the leg was probably the result of my pelvis having been out of alignment since birth. It meant I had always walked with more weight on my right leg than my left. The leg has severely restricted movement when I bend it back but it has never been something I have worried about, certainly nothing which has niggled at me mentally when I'm kicking.

The day I was born my dad, Ian, kicked five goals for Okato against Tukapa in the Taranaki club competition. My mother, Pam, had been in the home since Thursday. At noon on Saturday she told the obstetrician he'd better get cracking because her husband had a match to play and he couldn't play it sitting in the waiting room. The obstetrician said, "Him and me both. My son's playing for Tukapa and I can't watch him while I'm waiting for you." So they got cracking and produced me and dad went off happy and Okato stuffed Tukapa. You might say I had a kick-start to life. My folks say that when I was 18 months old they threw a ball to me across the room and I caught it. They judged that meant they had a natural on their hands. Parents are famously biased in these things. And usually wrong. Like mine.

I was not your naturally gifted kid. As I grew, I was nuts about sport – love wouldn't be too strong a word for it. Passion, even. But in many ways, physically, I didn't have what it takes to be the player to weave magic into a game instinctively, without any effort, in the way I imagine guys like Bryan Williams or Michael Jones or Grant Batty or Grahame Thorne did. What I did have was a compulsion to graft away until I got things right. And added to that I had what was probably an objectionable hatred of losing. Winning was everything.

When you talk about love of the game you are really talking about the environment in which you were part of the game as a child. In all my years with Auckland and with the All Blacks I have never forgotten the beginning of it all in what is the true heartland of rugby in New Zealand – out in the countryside on the rough paddocks where side-stepping is as much a matter of not putting your foot in something as it is of getting past the other joker.

Paradise – the posts, the paddock at Waotu.

Being born in Taranaki, the son of a dry-stock farmer whose heart, next to his family, was in the local rugby club was an advantage most city kids may not understand. The rugby club was the warm social centre of rural districts all around New Zealand. It was to the club's home paddock I was taken in a pushchair when all I understood about rugby was its bustle and noise, the serious look on dad's face and being dressed in woolly clothes to keep out the cold. Probably the first technical rugby term which meant anything to me was, "Aw, c'mon Okato! Get stuck in!"

From Taranaki we moved to Waotu, about 10 miles from Putaruru in southern Waikato. Waotu, as it was then in 1964 when I was two, was not too hard to find provided you had a keen eye and didn't miss the school and the garage as you shot through. It was home for 12 years and it was a gentle roll-over from the Okato footy club to Putaruru Athletic. Dad was one of those sound, reliable fullbacks who toe-kicked goals torpedo-style in the days before goal-kicking went circular and became the preserve of smart-arse little first five-eighths. He played for South Waikato in the Peace Cup before giving the game away in 1969. He reckoned that when they brought in the bounce-into-touch rule it was too late for an old dog to learn new tricks.

Seven or eight years later I watched him play at first five-eighths in an invitation match. He hadn't played competitive rugby for so long yet his touch was there and so were the essentials of technique when he kicked for goal. He landed four out of four, a couple of them from the touchline, and I felt all the old little-boy pride in him.

Both he and my mother were at the beginning of all sport for me and, later, for my brothers, Paul, 19 months younger than myself, and Brendan, five years younger. When you talk of "naturals" in sport, you talk of people like Paul. Everything came easily to him whether in rugby, in which he played equally well as flanker or hooker – well enough to play for Auckland when he could get on to the paddock over Sean Fitzpatrick's dead body – cricket, in which Lance Cairns said he could have represented New Zealand had he the mind to do it and golf, in which he achieved a single-figure handicap within four years.

Paul gave up rugby after a year and a half sitting in the stand waiting for Fitzy to break a leg, an arm, or anything. He decided he had better things to do with his life than accumulating bench splinters in the bum. Brendan played at first five-eighths and fullback and was intense and diligent about his sport. Between the three of us, we played more than 100 games for the Auckland Grammar first XV.

As with all farming families we worked hard together and

with the neighbours, whether it was haymaking or calf castration, mothering a rejected calf, rousing the sheep at shearing time, doing the lambing and calving beat with dad. Much the same as in sport, my intention to do things well on the farm was encouraged and I was never shooed away when I wanted to get in among the machines.

I loved the machinery. At the age of seven or eight I was standing up at the wheel of the Landrover, driving. Within three or four years I was driving tractors trailing mowers or balers. The open countryside was my oyster. I loved getting out and over the fences. No limits. No boundaries.

It was this willingness to give me my head which paid off for my father one horrendous day when I was, I suppose, 11. I remember it was the year of the beef crash when cattle dad had bought and farmed for 12 months were suddenly worth hardly the grass they had grazed on. It was a desperately difficult time for us. Dad and I were the only ones on the property this day and he decided to get to work on a paddock of calves which had to be castrated. He was a dab hand with a scalpel and the work was going well when one of the calves, not surprisingly considering what he was being deprived of, lashed out. There was no kick rail, the hoof slammed into the scalpel driving it into dad's chest and followed through to knock him semi-conscious.

The scalpel took an artery below the shoulder. There was a frightening gush of blood, then a steady pumping. Dad came-to sufficiently to staunch the blood with his singlet and somehow together we got to the Landrover. I drove like a bat out of hell across the paddock, down the road and up the neighbour's driveway. They applied pressure until the ambulance arrived from Tokoroa and not much more than an hour after it happened he was in hospital. Alone on the farm he would have died in the cattle yards.

I tell the story maybe less dramatically than dad would. The fact is that it was the confidence my parents had placed in me, from which I in turn took confidence, which meant that at that age I could drive him to help. For me, driving a Landrover was as much a satisfying job of work as kicking a barefoot goal over the Mickey Mouse goalposts I used to cobble together with scraps of timber from around the farm. Instead of thanking me mum and dad should have been congratulating themselves on an attitude which meant I had no parental barriers to overcome in my enthusiasm to do all the things they did.

Tennis, cricket, soccer, rugby, golf...we knocked about at all of them. I wouldn't let up – or couldn't let up – in any of our games until I could, at least, make a good fist of giving mum and dad a go or, at best, match them or beat them. If I was hit around in our

The big-time – boots and a full-size ball. Gwynne Shield team with dad extreme left and me fourth from left at the front.

cricket matches I got wild. If I missed shots at goal I was decidedly morose. If we lost a footy match I was very, very scratchy. Somehow everything was a contest that had to be won. Even then I was living for the day when I would be an All Black, for if one thing burned more fiercely in my heart than any other, it was that ambition. Well, that and sometime playing in my first pair of boots.

Those were the beautiful, painful barefoot days when the temperature dipped far down into low single figures and the frost still sat in a crust on the ground when you played and if you complained about the cold you were a woofter. I didn't lace on a footy boot until I was 13 when I made the Gwynne Shield team. Boots and a full-size footy ball! I knew at last I had made the big time. I guess Ian Wood had much the same sort of ten-foot-tall complex out at centre in the same team. He was a gifted, gutsy footballer then just as he was to become for Manawatu, Auckland and North Harbour. No wonder the Aussie league scouts liked what they saw. Along with my father Ian's dad, Dave, who had been an outstanding five-eighths for Waikato in the 1960s, was a constant presence and had a big influence on the kids growing up around Putaruru.

Incidentally, another, older kid growing up in Putaruru in the late 1960s was the son of the proprietors of the only 24-hour service station between Auckland and Wellington. His name was

Smith. Wayne Smith. As a barefooter before my time at primary school in Putaruru then fully-booted at Putaruru High School, Wayne made quite a name for himself among the locals. In 1984 I was to shadow him, now a polished, beautifully-balanced footballer, into the All Blacks for the Fiji tour, then Argentina and then, of course, we became Cavaliers...but that's another story.

Even when I was six or seven I was knocking nails into unlikely scraps of wood from around the farm so that I would have something to kick at. It was some sort of masochistic trip, too, because place-kicking a ball with bare toes on a cold day was not something anyone did for laughs. But it forced me to kick with either foot. When my right toe got really sore I kicked with my left until that got really sore by which time my right had recovered sufficiently to take some more punishment. You might call it a vicious cycle, but the satisfaction of it outweighed the pain.

In successive years, 1970 and 1971, when I was eight and nine, three events occurred which, when stitched together, created a new launch-pad for my rugby. The first involved only myself. I was sick of having sore toes.

The second involved a young New Zealander playing with sensational brilliance in South Africa. Bryan Williams, even on the small black-and-white screen, made such a vivid impact on an impressionable mind that he filled my thoughts then and for years afterward. I guess he became the hero of thousands of eight-year-olds, but I'd bet that in none of them did that hero-worship burn as brightly as in me. Immediately, I had to have a black jersey and black shorts. Mum understood the urgency. She cut a fern and number 13 from a white sheet and from then on that was my uniform for the front lawn and, I suspect, for bed. I have reflected on it often and I know that my ambition to be an All Black was fired by the Williams of 1970.

My first live look at Beegee was my first experience of actually being at a test. It was the infamous "Lake Eden" test against Scotland in 1975. We stood at the back of the terraces. My gumboots filled with rainwater and I didn't care because Beegee still had those magical qualities, far too much dynamite for the Scots, unstoppable even in water that seemed to lap at his kneecaps. In 1982 when I first played with him for Auckland he was a veteran and, obviously to anyone else, much of that incredible bursting vitality was just a memory. But to me he was still the 1970 Williams, scoring that fabulous try in the last test at Ellis Park.

The third event involved a Welshman in Lions' clothing. Barry John's round-the-corner instep kicking in 1971 fascinated me. He just never seemed to miss. There was more to him than

The man my toes saluted – Barry John.

that...his judgement of the tactical kick, his uncanny ability to bounce the ball into touch at will. But for a little kid with sore toes his kicking round the corner was a revelation. So I went out and just did it. I didn't think about the complications of it. I went out on to the front lawn with a size four ball and ten bare toes and did it. For hours. And my toes saluted Barry John.

I hounded dad to build some real posts – y'know, dad, real posts. They went up on the Waotu property and they are there to this day, though the family has long since moved over to the Bay of Plenty. I would kick at those posts until my legs were dropping off and then, for a change, I'd get out an old seven-iron and use the posts for target practice.

After the Gwynne Shield it was on into the Roller Mills competition, the stepping-stone through the years for so many bright prospects, and then into the Waikato schoolboys team as a second five-eighths to play Auckland schoolboys on Eden Park. It would be nice to talk about the first awesome experience of playing on Eden Park before 40,000 tumultuous spectators. I would lie. We were the curtain-raiser to the curtain-raiser to the main event. It was 11am and 50 roaring fans watched a Pacific Islander named Trevor White do me like a dinner on the inside thrust, run 70 metres and score. We lost 8-4 and I have never heard of Trevor White since, which seems to me to be a hell of a pity.

Through the years I played at schoolboy level, and even beyond, there were Islanders and Maoris of stunning ability, players of power and high skill with such promise of big futures. So many of them have come to nothing as rugby players and while that may not appear on the surface to be momentous there is significance in it. Certainly a proportion of those boys have drifted away from rugby – and away from all sport. That this is a drain on the talent-in-depth aspect of the game is secondary to the loss it is to the boys themselves. Through the schools and clubs rugby is New Zealand's greatest social and racial equaliser – and we can't deny there is a desperate need for a medium through which the races can come together in a warm social environment. Almost by tradition the rugby clubrooms of New Zealand have become our most active vehicle to that end.

As a student at Auckland Grammar I was decidedly middle stream. Gone were the 11-year-old's romantic notions about becoming a fighter pilot. Physics proved to be not quite my gig, anyway, and I guess that has been the eventual stumbling block for thousands of 11-year-old air aces who fought brilliant dogfights in their minds as they battled against sleep. Having been deemed not intelligent enough to go into the classical Latin stream I had the choice of studying French or Japanese. I opted for Japanese, five years of it.

Before the All Blacks went to Japan in 1987 I did a crash refresher course with a Japanese photographer who came to New Zealand to cover the World Cup and I envisaged the stunned admiration of the other players as I stepped in as interpreter. In the event, no fluent Fox interpretations. No stunned admiration. Japanese is not just Japanese singular. Japanese is a language with many different characters and characteristics. When we arrived and I saw all these Chinese characters I was, to put it mildly, stuffed. However, I did make a hit with the autograph-hunters when I was able to write their names in Japanese.

My first taste of first XV rugby came in the fourth form when the Grammar team to tour Fiji was announced. There were two Foxes at the school, the other a lock named Andy, and when the name was called we both went up hopeful and embarrassed. It happened they had enough locks and not enough first five-eighths. Gary and Alan Whetton and John Mills were there, big hairy guys who actually shaved! I'm not sure my voice had even

The kid with the chicken legs, Auckland Grammar first XV. Mike Thomas, with human legs, considers his options.

Winter and summer of content at Grammar. The first XV and the first XI of 1980. Top: Marty Crowe, try-scoring winger, third from left middle row. Bottom: Grant Fox, first-change bowler, third from right, front row. Mark Greatbach, third from left, back row.

broken and I hadn't a hair in sight south of my skull. Very intimidating.

Fiji was a tour I wouldn't have gone without. Over on the island of Levuka the local team had no use for boots so we played bare-footed, too. The field was jumping with toads. Stepping on one was a diverting experience, not just for the unique sensation on the sole of the foot but for the belching gasp the toads gave as they breathed their last. It became a contest between three teams, the Fijians, the New Zealanders and the toads. Regrettably, the toads ran a long last. The Fijians were a more impressive second and the New Zealanders won well.

In that match I kicked bare-footed without discomfort – and this might be an appropriate time to resolve what, through the years, has been a matter of considerable debate, expert rugby comment and even medical opinion. My preference for wearing the lightest boots possible has exercised some of the most brilliant minds of the media but I cannot recall ever being asked why. I wear light boots because that is the closest I can get to wearing bare feet, the closest I can get to physical contact with the ball. If that makes me some sort of nut-case, so be it.

We had a fiery game at Buckhurst Park in Suva. I had already suffered from and appreciated deeply the physical hardness of the young Fijians. I was a midget among giants. But at Suva it was something else. It was projectile rugby: Pass, duck and hope the human missile flies over the top. The whereabouts of the ball, usually of some passing interest in a game of rugby, seemed of no special consequence.

Ten minutes before the scheduled end of the game there was a mass declaration of discontent on one 22. On the other 22 a couple of us and a couple of Fijians grazed contentedly as the fighting surged. As a spectacle it left something to be desired scientifically but for enthusiasm and serious intent it scored straight As. The referee thought it decidedly below average as a scrap and called the whole show off. Such was my introduction to first XV rugby. Officially, it was recorded as disgraceful conduct unbecoming of the sons of gentlefolk and a blot on the Grammar escutcheon. Behind closed doors, however, there was great interest in the intrinsic quality of the brawl.

I was a student just good enough to get School Certificate in six subjects, have University Entrance accredited and to win a B bursary. You may think that qualified me for a lofty career as an academic but that would ignore the peculiar Fox priorities. I stayed back for my seventh form year to play rugby and cricket. A professional schoolboy. If that means I was abusing the education system I apologise in retrospect, but not with much conviction.

Cricket in the summer was as absorbing for me as rugby in winter. As a team game it was second in my affections but as a game to play probably third to rugby and tennis. I was useful enough as a first-change bowler of round-arm medium-paced skidders-cum-outswingers and number six or seven batsman to hold a place in the Grammar first XI for a couple of years. The Grammar years were the beginning of a close and lasting friendship with Martin Crowe, who was to become New Zealand's cricket captain and a world record-breaking batsman.

He was a freak all-round sportsman. In 1979 he played in the first soccer XI. In 1980 he switched to rugby and went straight into the first XV as a winger. I have no doubt that had he gone on with his rugby he would have become a top player in any company. He was big, fast, read the game swiftly and had the try-scoring instinct. He scored three in a match against St Paul's; there were the qualities there of a game-breaker. We were intense head-to-head contestants. Whether in our two-man cricket tests in the prefects' common-room or goal-kicking tests on the footy field we went at it like bitter enemies. In our slogging matches with stump and tennis ball we shattered common-room windows, the concentration of other prefects of a more circumspect turn of mind and the patience of the caretaker who had to repair the windows. It was, at the time, highly gratifying.

In that seventh form year we turned to classes as a casual gesture and to sport as a duty. Martin became the salaried groundsman that year but he couldn't drive a tractor. I could. Without official sanction, I took over that responsibility and we rolled the cricket pitch till it shone, a hard, flat, grassless strip, then prayed for divine approval at toss time. When we got it, which, surprisingly, was often, Martin always batted and his flow of great innings became a talking point far beyond the walls of Grammar.

His bowling at that level could be devastating, too, but he contends I had a hand in that. By that time my family had moved to Te Puke to become kiwifruit orchardists and, down there on holiday, Martin and I were pruning a shelter-belt. Mostly, we did the orthodox thing and pruned the trees but as a light variation I pruned a chunk out of Martin's right index-finger with the chainsaw. He hated the sight of blood so did not find that sort of rustic surgery greatly amusing at the time. However, the scars, physical and mental, healed over and he swears now that the changed structure of the finger improved his bowling no end. Somehow, he had to come out of it a winner.

As tennis partners we were more in your antagonistic McEnroe mould than your refined Edberg. We treated the ball brutally but without much style, our touch more excruciating than exquisite.

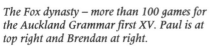

The Fox dynasty – more than 100 games for the Auckland Grammar first XV. Paul is at top right and Brendan at right.

Using the McEnroe bullyboy approach to cow the true stylists we made it through to the school final. Back in the fourth form we had played the junior final against Bruce Derlin, an ebullient character who was to become a New Zealand Davis Cup player. I say we played Derlin because he told his little partner to crouch at the net and keep his head down. Then he played us on his own. We were leading in the first set when the light got bad and Bruce wanted to call it off. Marty was highly indignant and wouldn't hear of it. Bruce came back strongly into the game. The light deteriorated marginally. Marty picked up his bag and went home.

When we played singles against each other it was not a spectacle for the weak of stomach. It was gamesmanship carried to the limit, each trying to out-McEnroe the other. It hasn't changed. I anticipate our final grudge match when we are in our late 80s, loser pays for the coffins.

Just to round out the young-Fox sporting bit...the summer of the first year I left Grammar I trained my little guts out preparing for my first year of senior rugby for University. Sly Stallone bashing sides of beef and running a million miles as he trained for his world title fight in the first of the interminable Rocky series had nothing on me. The winter of 1981 was a giant step out of rugby adolescence into adulthood and my intention to be ready for it was obsessive. That meant no cricket and because I loved the game it was no small sacrifice.

The next summer I spent working at the orchard in Te Puke, joined the local cricket club and met one of the most engaging men I have known in sport, Andy Roberts, who had played for New Zealand in the '70s, and who was to die so tragically young. He asked me what I did. I said I sort of bowled, y'know, sort of first-change stuff. He watched me bowl in the nets and asked kindly, "Can you bat?" Well, I said, I batted six or seven for Grammar. So he batted me at three. We had a useful sort of partnership in a one-day game and I stayed at first-drop.

After playing for Bay of Plenty Colts I got a game for the senior team against a touring Australian club side which had a quicky who was pretty sharp and had us 8-3 in no time. The sledging was running hot, real Aussie stuff full of delicate witticisms and subtle repartee. First slip: "Where the f— did they find you, shorty?" Second slip: "Down a Dandenongs dunny, eh, har-har-har." Wicket-keeper: "Where did you learn to bat, sonny?" Silly mid-off: "The amputee training school. Har-har-har." So I got a bit hosed-off with the whole show and picked up the quicky off a full length with that classical cricket stroke, the mid-wicket smash across the line with plenty of bottom hand. Not what you might call elegant, not your technically-precise despatch a la

Martin Crowe – my bitter opponent, my close friend.

Crowe, but on the fullish length this chap was bowling it proved consistently fruitful. Ugly but fruitful. I got to 60-odd and the following summer had a regular place in the Bay of Plenty team. We played Northland for the right to challenge Nelson for the

Hawke Cup. They had this old bandy-legged joker named Bob Cunis, who had been a great warhorse for New Zealand and who could still be sharpish but, most irritating of all, hit the seam five balls out of six. Other than to launch the occasional fully-pitched one back over his head I just couldn't get my bat to him. After I'd played and missed yet again, he put his hands on his hips, glared down the pitch and demanded, "Where the bloody hell did they find you? Out in the bush?" I couldn't think of an adequate answer. It was at least a prettier compliment than the Aussies could manage.

We won the match with a bit of Andy Roberts psychology. We scored 240-odd and had them 239-9. Andy brought on his off-spinner and we thought he had suddenly lost his marbles. He set the field. The spinner ran in. Andy stopped him and ostentatiously waved the mid-wicket fieldsman out to the boundary. Well, I thought, at least that makes a bit of sense. The bowler ran in again. Andy, looking very apologetic, stopped him and gesticulated at mid-wicket, bringing the fieldsman back into the orthodox position. The batsman sighed, looked meaningfully toward the boundary, took guard, went for the big hoick over mid-wicket, missed and was bowled.

We played Nelson on the Trafalgar Park track which must have had more runs scored on it than any other in the world. Batting in Paradise, they call it. Nelson was riding high in those days with a team including the Englishman Richard Hayward and actual or future New Zealand players in Jock Edwards, Andrew Jones and Tony Blain. Batting first they got 480 plus a few with Hayward, Edwards and Blain hitting centuries.

Andy Roberts' tactical talk was deeply analytical: "If you want to win the Hawke Cup don't get hit on the pads." He batted beautifully for 50, was hit on the pads and was out. Andrew Jones rolled up one of those gentle little pretend-spinners to me. I thought, "you can go over cow-corner," gave it a heave and was bowled. The Hawke Cup was safe for the zillionth time and the following Sunday all of Nelson praised the Lord for bestowing upon the province many bountiful gifts, the richest of which was the Trafalgar Park pitch.

I write of cricket not because I was a champion at the game, far from it, but because it was so much a part of my life at that time. My winters in Auckland, coming to grips with the new intensity of rugby at senior and, then, representative level were demanding. My summers in Te Puke, playing cricket in that lazy rural atmosphere, were the sublime relaxant, yet the challenge I demanded for myself was still there. The one-on-one match between batsman and bowler satisfied the need I felt for contest in whatever sport I played.

2

A different planet

Oh hell. Here's trouble. We're thin on the ground out there. Christ, it's Campo. It's Campo running like a blue-arsed fly. We're in double-shit. He's flat-stick across our defence. Now there's only JK. Stay out or come in? Campo's into the hole. JK's lunging, grabs his arm. Too late. Campo's laughing. Seven minutes. Australia 4, New Zealand 0. The Brit newshounds will love this.

Not like 1987. Four years on now, playing on foreign soil. Different players, different strokes. Different, different, different. A great year, 1987. Vintage. What was I in 1987? Three years as an All Black but a tyro still. Enough of a kid at 24 to be wondering sometimes by what dream-sequence of events I should be plucked up and dropped in among all these great players, to be part of a magic team. It was as if the demi-deity in charge of Kids With Ambition had latched on to me because I was easy to pick out – the talkative brat with the snowy hair – and smoothed the way.

There I was. Aucklander by choice, country boy at heart. I still am. I remember going back to the farm on holiday, riding the farm-bike up to the top of the hill beyond the woolshed and sitting there for hours deep in contemplation of absolutely nothing. It was everything the country balladeers sing about. A whisper of breeze, crisp smell of hay, birds making music. Most of all, the deep peace of it. Poetic, eh? This is me, I said. This is really me. So like several million other country kids around the world I breathed it all in and went back to the city. When I left Auckland Grammar I worked on the old man's kiwifruit orchard through the summer. At the end of it I told him I was going back to Auckland for the footy season. He reasoned with me, quietly presenting the case for the country. Why go back there and get swallowed up? Wouldn't it be better to stay here and take your chances where it's a bit easier? That made a lot of sense to me. I chewed it over for five seconds and slung my hook back to Auckland. No offence, dad, honest. But y'know.

An attraction was that my old Grammar coach, Graham Henry, was coaching the University Club. He was the great encourager, the quiet persuader. He gave me my groundwork in organisation, options and tactics. His approach to rugby was very structured with clean-cut patterns. He instilled the requirement to think constantly, to out-think the opposition, to place yourself mentally in a dominating position. Organisational rugby with flexible overtones.

Graham's first five-eighths and second five-eighths stood still as part of his pattern. I never questioned that. I am sure it was what he judged to be the most effective means of moving the ball wide quickly. In target plays, however, we ran on to the ball. The years have rolled by and some commentators – and the old All Black five-eighths Earle Kirton in particular – have been critical of the static-platform distribution I have tended to use from first five-eighths in the All Blacks. I believe the skill factor is high while standing still – much higher than distribution on the run. In those days before such sophistications as drift defences and Bob Dwyer, Graham was the coach who taught me it was not good enough just to go out and play a game of footy. Game plans, homework, the analysis of opposition strengths and weaknesses, an overall pattern fine-tuned match by match for different opponents...he conducted a university of rugby. It was a university to which, shamelessly, I applied myself with more diligence than I did that other, academic, institution which was supposed to be moulding me – with minimal help from myself – into a finely-rounded individual with a future in commerce. Between Varsity and footy I had an upkeep cushion through some part-time work in the sports shop of Merv Wallace, whose stature as a New Zealand cricketer I did not fully understand until I heard his peers and his students speak of him with reverence. He also had a daughter named Adele. Working alongside her, I found the merchandising trade becoming increasingly attractive.

Part-time with Merv became full-time when I kicked university to touch, a hell of a kick, long, spiralling, out of sight and out of mind. What I was doing was choosing a diploma in rugby, a qualification not so far recognised by cap and gown and drinking horns but, I reckoned, a great door-opener in a country like New Zealand. If, in the rugby context of that era, that seemed quaintly mercenary for a kid still wet behind the ears, maybe it was just that I was some years, but not many, ahead of my time.

Campo the incomparable – he meant trouble.

My first year of senior club rugby was also my first conscious introduction to the bitterness, the rage, the divisiveness, the sadness resulting from political morality becoming inextricably entangled in what I had thought to be rugby's own world. My view of the 1981 South African tour of New Zealand was, of course, simplistic. I was a young man who believed in rugby through and through. I could not contemplate any situation which could make the great national sport a vehicle for such political protest that the people would be at each other's throats.

I could not accept that by organising a rugby tour the New Zealand Rugby Union was condoning or encouraging the political system of another country. I am acutely aware that the consequences of the tour were deeply harmful to rugby in New Zealand, but at the time I saw the right of protest abused by many I believed to be in it only for a crack at law and order. I debated with myself the nature of the protest by those who truly believed in the right of their cause. I could not rationalise their denial of the rights of those who favoured the tour with the point of their protest, which was against the denial of rights to the black people of South Africa.

I wanted to know more about protesters' stances on the desecration of human rights in other countries with which we traded and played sport. What was the degree of selective morality involved in this? My attitude was no more and no less than the attitude of so many New Zealanders who neither marched nor stayed away from the games. And, to get down to the grass-roots reality of it all, as the politicians keep saying, I wanted to see the All Blacks stuff the Springboks. I also wanted to see Naas Botha kicking. And I did not want the South Africans to be able to go home beaten but with the excuse that they were deprived because of the turmoil. Bottom line, I suppose.

Because of the sad state of the nation, mums steered their children away from rugby – and I suppose that happened whether or not the kids preferred to play rugby. Whatever happens my children will have the choice. If young Ryan wants to play rugby league or soccer or go running across country or ride a horse into a Bell Tea commercial he will do it with my blessing and that of his mother – who, by the way, used to be Adele Wallace. If our daughter, Kendall, plans a career in jelly-wrestling we may gently point her toward something slightly less demeaning, like mud-wrestling, but that would involve only a little fine tuning.

I played rugby at Eden Park on September 12, 1981. That Day. The day of the barbed wire, the mindless buzzing of the players and the crowd by a pilot who, given an engine defect or an error on his own part, might have dived into thousands of innocent people. Auckland Colts played Counties Colts in the unreal atmosphere which preceded the totally bizarre. It is a game which will be remembered by none except the players who performed in front of the biggest crowd of their young lives, behind barbed wire and with police patrolling the touchlines. My memory of the game is dim; of the occasion, vivid.

Watching the test I was petrified that light plane would go out of control but not so petrified that I could not rise up and shout my thanks when Allan Hewson, with that dainty approach and fluent kicking style, landed the goal that won the match.

The following year I would be back on Eden Park as part of John Hart's Auckland team. Nineteen years old, still with a mountain of learning to do, my mental gear tuned into rugby at club pace, I just doubted myself a little. I couldn't quite accept that I belonged among his Auckland elite. It was not that I did not want to be there among the guns but that, somehow, I felt a bit embarrassed about it...Joe Stanley and Mike Mills, Gary Cunningham and Greg Burgess, Glenn Rich and the two guys who had locked the scrum in the Eden Park test against the Springboks, Andy Haden and Gary Whetton. Was this really the Whetton I'd played with at Grammar? He looked the same except for a bundle of hair on his top lip and Louis Moolman's scalp

Bryan Williams – from childhood hero to Auckland team-mate.

hanging from his belt but this Whetton was an All Black who had played against and beaten the Springboks. And then Harty pulled in Bryan Williams and I thought, what the hell am I doing on the same planet as this guy?

So even without having stepped into the ring I had manoeuvred myself on to the ropes. Between seasons I had experimented with my goalkicking, aiming to reduce the right-to-left swing by kicking straight through the ball rather than sweeping it. I felt it was paying dividends. So goalkicking was not at the core of my worries. It was just being there, I suppose. Inevitably, then, I found the early days of representative rugby difficult.

There were a couple of losses which I felt deeply. I had the feeling the team was not really gelling and I fretted about my own contribution to the problems. I wasn't being slagged-off by the critics but I questioned my own input. I didn't try to rationalise my own performances with my inexperience. Although I was aware I was not really the sort of player who would come into a team at this level and make a dynamic impact, I had been picked to do a key job at representative level. I had to perform. When we lost a match to Canterbury I "knew" we should have won I put my head on the block for voluntary execution. I went to John Hart, poured it all out, told him I desperately wanted to play for Auckland and that it was in me to do the job he wanted but I needed help. What he gave me back was reassurance. He told me he hadn't selected me as a one-off gamble. He had selected me because he believed in me as an investment. At this stage, he said, he still owed me. He wasn't about to pull out of his investment when he could sense it was about to pay a dividend.

So he sent me back out there and we won and went on winning right through to the National Championship. I don't know how many other players might have gone to Harty in the same frame of mind as myself. Maybe none. But I do know that had they, he would have given them much the same response. In effect, he was backing his judgement by giving players a fair number of games to prove themselves. I became more focussed on my game, now conscious that the step up from club to representative level was more a matter of getting my head together than of suddenly sprouting wings or growing muscles where my brain used to be.

When I went into Harty's squad I knew him by reputation as Waitemata's halfback, a feisty, non-stop talker. What I found was a man in absolute control of training sessions, always talking but always encouraging, very rarely the terse word and then only to the individual he knew could handle it. He knew almost by instinct the ones who needed an ego massage, the ones who needed just a nod and a wink, the ones who would react

Lindsay Harris – "So sorry, Foxy, no advice."

positively to a gentle shafting. He was crystal clear setting out his requirements to the team and to individuals. No room for doubt and none for excuses if his strategy was ignored. What he wanted from me was not very different from what Graham Henry had wanted. What he gave me was the confidence that I belonged.

The nature of the contest for positions in the Auckland team had not really occurred to me until I went to Lindsay Harris after marking him in a trial match. As a gesture of respect and as the new kid on the block, I asked him if he had any advice to give me on my performance that day. Lindsay eyed me without favour. "Listen," he said, "you want to play for Auckland, I want to play for Auckland. You want to play first-five eighths, I want to play first five-eighths. You get no help from me." And he finished his drink, poured another and changed the subject. On reflection, I understood what he was saying and respected it. Lindsay was to play most of his rugby for Auckland at fullback and, given the day and the occasion, he was just brilliant, irrepressible, combative, inventive, putting his own distinctive mark on rugby.

That's what it's about, this game. While fulfilling the team patterns, the pre-ordained strategies, the organisation, there must always be a place for the instinctively brilliant player to express himself. I doubt that Australia truly appreciated until very recently what they had in David Campese, never knew quite what part to give him in a game. Consequently Campo became his own man, somehow removed from the grand plan. He could be devastatingly good. He could be devastatingly bad and, to Australia's disadvantage, he was too often judged on the bad – on the waywardness, the pass into oblivion, the occasionally weak concentration under the high ball. His status as a game-breaker did not seem to be harnessed into target-areas, rather left to Campo to pull it off when all else had failed.

That is the past. Campo, the Godfather kid of our Colts days, is now a national treasure, given freedom but pulled into the team plays as a planned missile. That mind-boggling first try in the World Cup was a case in point. I would bet my right foot or even my right anything – yes, even that – that it was a planned call when Campo hissed across from his right wing to pick up on that Aussie move which had started at the lineout Willie-away they do so effectively using Nick Farr-Jones, progressed to Michael Lynagh's superbly set-up second-phase ball and finished with Campo slashing back, flat across our sketchy defensive line and putting the ball down for the try on the left flank.

In fact, I wonder a bit whether some of us didn't have a hand in Campo's release from solitary. Perhaps the Aussies learned from the Northern Hemisphere-Southern Hemisphere match preceding the sevens at Hong Kong last year that a Campese given the ball as part of a team strategy to bring him into the play while discarding his reputation for unreliability would pay off in gold.

3

The first fern

Lineout. Ruck. Switch direction. Lynagh's shoved a kick through. He's found space. Crowley or Campo? Campo or Crowley? Oh hell, it's bounced for Campo. He's got Timu on the wrong foot. Zinzan's got him. Good old Zinny. Look out for Horan. Campo can't pass from there. Bullshit. Today Campo can do anything. He's flicked it up and over his shoulder like a mad juggler. Horan's clear. Campo's laughing again. Thirty-four minutes. Australia 13, New Zealand 0. Claw-back time.

Claw-back time has been pretty much a rarity for All Black teams through the masterful years of the '80s. Scotland and Australia have given us a recent taste of it, if not for it, but mostly trying to catch up in a match has been for the other jokers. The skill and the will – 30 per cent of skill, 70 per cent of will – to fight back from desperate situations is, mercifully, built in to New Zealand rugby players from the time they understand that winning is a warmer feeling than losing. Pride is the most powerful element as children become young men at college and as young men become provincial and national representatives. A match is never lost until the referee declares it's time for a few beers under the stand.

You speak of claw-back or fight-back and you speak of that magnificent day for rugby at Lancaster Park in 1985 when, by the saving grace of John Kirwan's fingertips, Auckland took the Ranfurly Shield from a Canterbury rampantly coming back from 24-0 at halftime to lose 28-23. It was a day for everyone. All of Canterbury and a fair bit of Auckland squeezed into Lancaster Park. The noise from the stands and the embankments was the noise that first fills then dominates the senses.

It was the day the Canterbury coach, Grizz Wyllie, was

Celebrating one of rugby's greatest adventures – Andy Haden, John Hart, Alan Whetton and Gary Whetton with the Ranfurly Shield won from Canterbury in the 1985 classic.

obstructed and manhandled by some decidedly ill-advised ya-hoos as he went on to the ground at halftime to deliver what everyone assumed would be a rip-roaring rocket to the Canter-bury players. But this was a day for Grizz the philosopher. He pointed to the ball and said, "They scored 24 points with this. So can you." And they bloody nearly did.

We could not have done much more to assist the Canterbury cause. We sat on our lead, became defensive, a dangerous twist of tactics in any game of rugby let alone one against an angry Canterbury team defending a marvellous Ranfurly Shield record. They played the second half like shield challengers, we like shield defenders on a bad day – not as urgently fired-up as respectable shield defenders. Too casual, concentration levels down, too prone to wallow in our first-half cushion. Undoubt-edly the big comeback started with pride and then boiled with the exhilaration of the chase as that madly-Canterbury, won-derfully-rugby crowd bayed for Auckland blood. They got much more of it than we would have volunteered as donors. At the height of it all someone tossed a gory pig's head on to the field. Did it have some terrible ritual significance or was it a studied insult to the social shortcomings of the Auckland front row?

I don't actually wake in the night screaming as I see again Wayne Smith's final towering punt but I can still feel the dread as it hovers, so tantalising Lindsay Harris in the in-goal that he is unable to cover it. It was a great move by Smithy. We knew he would keep the ball in hand and he knew we knew and that we would move up in defence. When we obliged like puppets on the end of Smithy's string he hoisted that precision kick which, for him, was the expression of an art form.

The mad scramble in the Auckland in-goal as it fell to ground fuelled the crowd's fire as no other part of the Canterbury fight-back had.

Canterbury players following through for the kill and Auckland players in terror of being the victims arrived from all over the planet in a crazy contest for the ball. Auckland fingers got to it first and the ball careered into the dead zone. At first I was given credit for owning the fingers that won the shield. In fact, Kirwan climbed all over me in pursuit of that little piece of glory.

I'm sure Grizz still grumbles through his moustache about the legality of the tap-back into the dead-ball area and all of Canterbury bears the mental scars inflicted by the torture of the referee's final whistle.

What a game it was. What heroics. Impossible to believe as a piece of fiction. After all the test matches, all the triumphs and tragedies, that match stands out in my mind as a monument to rugby for within it was everything which makes the game great, a game not to be bastardised by law-makers who are tempted to turn it into something else because they fear what is not frightening. The scope is there, of course, for intelligent tuning to increase opportunity to run with the ball – and of course it is right to salute the ultimate achievement of the game by increasing the points for a try – but that is another story, another chapter.

By the time Auckland played Canterbury on Lancaster Park, 1985, my career had taken a turn or two. I had come through 1983 with a place in the North Island team and a Colts-eye view of Michael Lynagh kicking goals from all over the place as Australia beat New Zealand 26-18 in the under-21 international. Mark Finlay, the Manawatu fullback, kicked the goals for the New Zealand Colts that day and I made a humble contribution with a dropped goal.

That year I also took my life in my hands by backing myself to drop-kick a goal with the Auckland match against the British Lions just about at its death-knock and the Lions leading 12-10. The other Auckland backs rather preferred a move aimed at scoring by the posts. Our forwards were going like tigers and I reckoned the certainty of three points for a one-point lead was preferable to the mere possibility of a four-point lead. So I called

The droppy I dared not miss – 12-10 down against the Lions of 1983 with David Irwin (13) and Ollie Campbell on the charge.

the drop-kick. I didn't consider the prospect of a miss. I had a super passer of the ball in Tim Burcher. We were 15 metres from the Lions' line and had the scrum-feed. The ground was pretty shifty but, I mean to say, a man shouldn't miss from there, should he?

God, what if it had missed? What if the wild-eyed Irishman David Irwin had got a touch on it as he charged in? What if my left foot hadn't known what my right foot was doing? What if I had been distracted by a passing dog? What sensitive part of a first five-eighths would six backs in a pique and eight forwards in a blind rage have gone for first? Right. So they would. Had I thought of that at the time we would have gone for the try by the posts.

Some critics have said that my eventual selection for the All Blacks was pre-destined from the time Pinetree Meads gave me the nod for the North Island in 1983 and 1984, and especially so in 1984. The timing of the 1983 match at Blenheim seemed almost a challenge to players to declare their loyalty to their provinces. Eight of the original North Island selection withdrew for an interesting variety of reasons, some of which certainly would not have stood up to examination under a weak microscope. Pinetree had the North team for the first time. The previous year he had been deeply hosed-off watching South take North to pieces and he reckoned no team should have submitted to that sort of treatment as docilely as the North Island players.

I understand he judged the potential of my contribution to a team more positively than some others in high selectorial places and he backed me without reservation in 1983. The match was a personal triumph for Andy Haden. He commanded the field. When Alwyn Harvey went off injured Andy took over the direction of the North team. It was not just that he gave South a bath in the middle of the lineout. His control of play gave me a sharp new insight into the breadth of his knowlege and his capacity to think, to make judgements, in the heat of the match. And even more than that, he illustrated the manner in which a dominating personality can draw response from his players by the sheer power of presence. That match was a telling education for me quite beyond the role I had of selecting options with the ball delivered. North won 22-9 and my statistical contribution was a dropped goal following a free-kick.

And then in 1984 at Rotorua, Meads said, "Get out there and run the game, Foxy", but there was a difference. Where in Blenheim Kieran Crowley had taken the kicks, here, by chance, the job was mine. The All Black fullback, Allan Hewson, had been forced out of the game by injury. He was replaced by Lindsay Harris and the goalkicking came to me.

By now, John Hart had given me the confidence to run a backline at first-class level. Together we had ironed out the difficulties I had in my first year – difficulties, I might add, which were largely self-imposed by my reluctance or inability to deviate from some pre-set notions. Once I started absorbing Hart's tuition and understood more fully the quality of the players around me that particular mental block dissolved.

This meant that running the North Island backline was no big deal in my mind. But being given the goal-kicking opportunity was the key to my performance that day. Somehow it raised the adrenalin level and everything else slotted into place. At the end of it I had converted North's five tries and kicked three penalties of five. It was odd that our last three tries were scored almost on the same spot, inches in from the touchline. I could have used the same kicking mark for all three but I'm a superstitious little sod and I moved the mark by about 12 inches each time.

I had also to thank that extraordinary fitness guru Jim Blair for taking a hand when I was finding it difficult to relax with my goal-kicking. After Auckland's earlier match against Sydney, when I missed some simple kicks. Jim taught me how to adjust my breathing in that period of concentration before running in for the kick...breathe in for one second, out for one, in for two, out for two, in for three, out for three. It has become part of that ritual which takes too long for some sensitive viewers but which, to put it simply, is doing it my way within the time-frame set down by the rules. The hand-waggling habit is also a sub-conscious relaxant. It is intriguing to see kids copying it and if it helps, why not? The proprietors of my lunch-bar tell me that, watching on television, they turn on quite an act going through the pre-kick performance with me. So I'm an entertainer?

I felt so in control of my game that day at Rotorua, deeply involved but somehow detached. It was the sort of game all of us want to have all the time but which, for all the complicated reasons which make rugby and individuals what they are, too rarely experience.

If those years were a big deal for me, consider what they were for a young player who, when I was having my first season for Auckland, had never been heard of outside his dad's butcher shop and, going into the 1983 season, was playing third grade for Marist in Auckland. John Hart plucked up John Kirwan and put him down on the wing in his provincial team, he went on into the North Island team and the beginning of a career which has made him, in his explosive way, one of the legends of New Zealand rugby. Once his ambition was to own his own butcher shop but it's a long time now since he boned a forequarter or overweighed an undercut. He has cut up a few opponents in his time but he's still got all his fingers - and he needs them, as well as his toes, to check out his Pasta Productions bank balance every month.

When that master of pessimism George Orwell wrote his preview of 1984 he missed the bus on rugby. His suffocating 1984 had nothing to do with my 1984. For me, it was a launch-pad of a year. It was the year I went on a five-week tour of France, Britain and America with an Auckland team celebrating the union's centennial. It was the year John Hart's vision for Auckland rugby started to materialise, the game opening out into a wonderfully broad, expansive vehicle for 15 players. It was the year University won the Gallaher Shield, symbol of Auckland club rugby

John Kirwan – a butcher with all his fingers.

supremacy. It was the year in which I tasted an internal tour with the New Zealand Juniors – five matches for five wins. It was the year in which records went for a row of ashcans. I was able to score 310 points in the home first-class season – and I promise this is not the beginning of a recital of the statistics of my career. Statistics can sketch their own impersonal view of my life in rugby elsewhere in this book.

Enough for me to say that I have never considered numbers as some way of proving I'm better than another record-holder from another era. "Fox beats Don Clarke's record" is someone's else's way of relating what I have done to what Don Clarke did. New records should never be allowed to diminish the greatness of the record-holders of the past. When Don Clarke played rugby the game was much less the generous scoring spectacle it is now. Through my years they have compared my kicking statistics with those of Clarke, Fergie McCormick, Mick Williment, Joe Karam, Allan Hewson, Robbie Deans. It would be shameful were their immense contributions to rugby in their own time to be expunged along with their records. Probably no kicker in the history of the game made an international impact comparable with that of Clarke. He was some sort of colossus, the sort of player who had the administrators of other countries scurrying to their lawbooks to see how they could manipulate points to negate the advantage the All Blacks had with a goal-kicker like him. His sort of history can never fade merely because under different conditions 30 years, 60 years, 100 years later someone else wipes his numbers off the board.

Statistics are the trivia of rugby. The heart and soul of rugby is in the people playing it, the friendships, the warmth of the companionship after a win or loss. It is in the drawing together of a small nation like ours which, in recent years, has had little to cheer about other than through sport. It is in the challenge the game presents to its players, the test of character it sets up. It is a game to challenge the mind as importantly as the body. Its statistics are incidental, if not irrelevant, to the game as a game. And if that sounds like a load of idealistic cobblers, too bad. It is what I feel.

There was in 1984 another occasion of mild interest for me, my family and my friends. These three jokers Bryce Rope, Tiny Hill and Brian Lochore sent me to the tropical paradise of Fiji. Mild interest! Like hell. Their All Black team was to be named the day after I had scored a poultice of points for Auckland in a national championship match and it would be mock modesty if I said I was not hopeful of making the team. There had been so much media conjecture – some of it probably inspired – that the possibility I would go as Wayne Smith's understudy had actually penetrated.

The night before the team announcement I slept like a man with a date with the electric chair. My bladder kept kicking me and saying, "Get up, Foxy, get up, I have to go again." My head

Jock Hobbs, my first All Black captain – red-blooded orator.

kept telling me, "Forget it, Foxy, forget it. It's a pipe-dream. You're not ready." It was a lethal mix.

I spent the day of the announcement with Adele, then my fiancee, and she had pulled a party trick by inviting some of my friends over, among them Marty Crowe and Mark Greatbatch. By the time the announcement was due on television I was so saturated with pros and cons that when my name went up I was numb. Marty said something like, "GJ Fox? That's got to be a mistake." Then everyone was leaping about, drinking a bit of this and a bit of that, and here it was, the moment I had burned for all those years – the kid who idolised an All Black, the kid who dreamed of being one, the kid who made it his business in life to become one – and I was like some sort of zombie.

A zombie. That's how I felt when I took my first shot at goal as an All Black...Suva. October 17, 1984. New Zealand v President's XV...I hoist one to make the Fijian fullback stretch. It forces a five-metre scrum. Craig Green scores the try like the insatiable finisher he is. I make my mark and measure my run in some sort of daze. Oh, god. I can't move. Stop shaking, Foxy. Lift your foot, Foxy. I can't. Some bugger's nailed it to the ground...and an agonising mental hour passes before I actually get to the point where the foot makes contact with the ball. A rough preparation, but the strike is as sweet as a nut.

I had heard and read so much about the gulf between preparedness for club rugby and for provincial rugby and then between provincial and international rugby that I hadn't known quite what to expect here. So I geared myself up to what I considered to be red alert. It is as well I did. In this game the pace went up several notches, more because of what the All Blacks were doing than the opposition. It was a continual search for a way through a midfield cluttered with vagrant but aggressive Fijian forwards and that placed an increased tactical responsibility on me. Things were happening more quickly, more physically. While for Auckland John Hart demanded very high standards I was even more conscious of the need to do things efficiently at speed in the All Blacks.

It was a requirement made even more urgent by a piece of red-blooded oratory by the new All Black captain, Jock Hobbs, at half-time. A solicitor and a gentleman through and though, Jock might not have got away with this speech in a court of law but at the end of it I must say we, the accused, were crystal clear about our misdemeanours and the penalty if we did not mend our ways. Any lingering doubts which might have existed among northerners about Jock's capacity for captaincy at this level went up in a puff of brimstone. The response when play resumed was electric.

4

Of Cups and Cavaliers

Go Stevie, go Stevie, go Stevie, go. Pop songs in the middle of a World Cup match? No one's singing here, baby. Except, maybe, Bob Dwyer up in the stand. And probably Campo's humming a hit from his planet's top-20. It's the first minute of the second spell. The first minute of 40 on the claw-back scale. Stevie McDowell bunts off the Aussie forwards, sets us up for the big thrust at the line. Craig Innes muscles ahead. Ruck. Now it's on. Dammit. The bloody Aussies have conceded the penalty. A sitter. Three points. Better for them than six and better for us than none, so let's have them...

To talk about the 1991 Cup campaign is to talk about the 1987 Cup campaign and the years between, to talk about the changing face of New Zealand rugby and unchanging strategies still based on players no longer there. In hindsight, the loss of the 1991 semi-final to Australia was a loss also to strategies only loosely anchored to reality. It was a loss to a better-equipped team with a hard-nosed game plan. It was a loss to an administrative gaffe which virtually forced a twin-coach situation between men who, demonstrably, were not twins. It was a loss to injury and it was a loss to time.

The loss to time was inevitable. Those who could not predict it and, therefore, could not accept it when it happened, cast about indiscriminately for whipping boys. The result was one of the most vicious witch-hunts New Zealand sport has known and it deteriorated further into character-assassination by a public which, having come to the end of a long ego-trip on the back of the All Blacks, found that losing with grace was beyond it.

New Zealanders had become so used to the reflected glory that when it was snatched away they responded boorishly, petulantly. Certainly, in comparison with the players in the firing line, they lost gracelessly. It was sad – much sadder than the loss of the World Cup – that a magnificent era of New Zealand rugby should end with yesterday's heroes being maligned as today's villains, ridiculed as players and as men.

In my own case it was the culmination of a year or two of malicious rumour-mongering which exposed the gullibility of many New Zealanders, their eagerness to believe the worst even in the absence of reason or logic and certainly in the absence of fact. They were rumours picked up and circulated overseas then, ludicrously, repeated in print here when transmitted back from abroad. Had these things not been so hurtful to my wife and family I might have laughed them off. In the event, I couldn't.

The All Blacks had gone through 1987, 1988 and 1989 un-defeated. In 1990, I was quoted as saying the All Blacks would falter one day, adding "we're only human". Anyone might have made that statement. There was nothing clever about it, though possibly I sensed its inevitability more sharply than others and my suggestion we were only human might have been at odds with the view of those who construct international programmes. We had had an extra-special group of players together. Could we maintain our run when time was called for a centre like Joe Stanley or for second five-eighths like Warwick Taylor and John Schuster or a fullback like John Gallagher? Eras begin and end whatever the sport. Ours ended on Lansdowne Road, Dublin, in 1991. Fortunately some of the players in that World Cup squad will go on to create the next great era, which is as inevitable as the end of the last.

Yet significantly, in the 1991 World Cup we played at a level only bettered by the Australians. We might have played England five times and beaten them five times. We might have played Australia five times and beaten them once. Maybe twice...maybe. It was Australia's year, the peak of a mountain they had been climbing with great purpose for several seasons, learning on the way, discarding losses as lessons (something the All Blacks would never have got away with), building with a great sense of the practicalities of their mission, toward World Cup victory.

I went into the 1991 World Cup as a seasoned international player. I went into the 1987 World Cup as an international tyro, wet behind the ears, one test under my belt and that against Argentina in 1985 when Smithy had to withdraw. I had marked that marvellous player Hugo Porta who did not have one of his most marvellous days. This was regrettable for an Argentine team of quite mercurial qualities in the backs and in combative mood in the forwards.

Had I been overwhelmed at the prospect before the game I soon found that on this day Porta would not be throwing too

Hugo Porta – not at his best as my first test opponent in 1985 but still at it in the World Cup of 1987.

many scares into anyone, not even a novice. While that had comforting overtones I felt somehow that I had been deprived, as if in my first test match I needed, even deserved, Hugo to be at his very best. Rather than counting my blessings that he wasn't I rather resented it, I suppose.

And there was, of course, 1986. What happened in 1986 was in direct relationship to what happened in 1985 when the tour of Argentina was a replacement for the scheduled tour of South Africa, abandoned by order of the High Court. The background to and actuality of the Cavaliers tour of South Africa has been told at length, chewed on, digested by some, spat out by others, the players praised, reviled. The most lasting repercussion was suspicion that we had all returned to New Zealand as rand millionaires or close to it. We did not. I did not. I have had to work just as hard to make a living since 1986 as I did before. Harder, in fact.

Because the Cavalier tour was a critical part of my career it is important in my story to set out my personal attitude to it. When the original, and aborted, Cavaliers tour was planned I said I would not be part of it. On that basis Frano Botica lined up. I would not go because I did not want my career to end on Loftus

A goal-kicker's dream – on the high veldt.

Versfeld. I suppose I was as angry as most All Blacks about the abandonment of the official tour and the means taken to squash it but I was not ready to gamble my rugby-playing future by taking part in an unsanctioned tour. Given time I changed my mind. Given time I listened and became angrier still. My future still meant as much to me but I was able to place the possible consequences in perspective.

The strong word was out that the action to halt the 1985 tour originated from the highest echelons of government. I was made aware that in the view of many people of the law the decision to scotch the tour was unsustainable. I did not, and do not, believe that by going on the tour I was condoning or supporting apartheid. Had that linkage occurred to me as in any way feasible I would not have gone but to me it was so tenuous as to be non-existent. The most persistent criticism was that by going on tour we were throwing the country back into the awful abyss of 1981,

First time in the city and first camera-experience for this Kalahari bushman and his family, Ellis Park, Johannesburg, 1986.

that it would yet again sour parents and encourage them to steer their children away from the game, that by going we were striking against our own game. Every one of us had rugby at heart. Every one of us believed rugby the game had been dealt an injustice. In my mind the injustice against rugby rankled as deeply as the injustice I perceived to myself.

What we learned was that thousands upon thousands of New Zealanders listened in the small hours to commentaries of our games. There was a measure of support for what we had done which was far greater than the correspondence columns and the editorials showed.

For New Zealanders the greatest challenge in rugby remained the defeat of South Africa in South Africa. We had been deprived even of confronting that challenge, let alone beating the Springboks. Now we were in South Africa wearing jazzed-up uniforms which said we were not the All Blacks but in our hearts it was as All Blacks we wanted – needed – to win the series of matches against the Springboks. That we were not able to do that was to us the greatest tragedy of the tour. Personally, I felt more fear of failure than ever before, more fear of failure than I have since. That was a reflection both of the overwhelming nature of the South African challenge to all New Zealand rugby and of our need to win. The feeling was that if we could win the so-called tests our actions would be vindicated – perhaps, even, that we could then more fully vindicate our actions to ourselves. Otherwise, we would be condemned. Success meant triumph. Failure meant retribution.

Retribution came. We were banned for two tests. Sections of the public and the media were infuriated by what they saw as "a slap on the wrist". We were advised we could win a court appeal against the sentence. We declined, not because we believed we had escaped lightly but because it would have been further trauma for the game.

The intensity of the contest on the field in South Africa raised my hackles. The matches were as grimly fought as true tests and only someone who has been to test matches in South Africa can know what that means. Playing against Naas Botha was a personal challenge. I sucked inspiration from it just as I sucked confidence from constant rugby against opposition that was invariably hard and sometimes harsh. The precision demanded of a first five-eighths was rammed home to me by the conditions, especially on the high veldt, and by such hardened campaigners as Andy Haden, Murray Mexted, Gary Whetton, Mark Shaw, Gary Knight, John Ashworth. They demanded the kick-off should be at the height and length they needed it to use it effectively as an attacking weapon. They demanded pin-point accuracy from the bomb. They demanded touch-kicks found touch. In that thin atmosphere failure to find touch meant you suffered a 70-metre touch-finder in response, and much the same if the kick-off was too deep or the bomb arrived 10 metres ahead of the followers.

Senior players among the backs, Dave Loveridge, Bill Osborne, Bernie Fraser, Warwick Taylor required accuracy in the calling of moves. I was playing in the midst of a great storehouse of rugby knowledge and I was learning from it.

Kicking goals in South Africa should be the dream of every goal-kicker in the world. For some, New Zealanders notable among them, it has been a nightmare. I tried to fathom why All Black goal-kickers have had such an embarrassing failure-rate in South Africa. Because everything worked for me, I could not. Finally, I put it down to the stress of playing for success in that country. I am sure prolific scorers like Laurie Mains, Fergie McCormick, Bob Scott succumbed to the mental rather than the physical pressures of playing in South Africa. That mental pressure transmitted itself to a physical incapability to follow the technical rules. Mental tension became physical tension and physical tension eroded technique. The Cavaliers tour gave me the capacity to isolate my goal-kicking from my general field play so that playing well was not dependent on kicking well. In a sense it was my giant step into international rugby. From being a guy who might have got into touring parties without demanding a test place, I came back to New Zealand with the sort of edge to my rugby which was to make me a test player by right...but not a test player immediately. The ban and Frano Botica took care of that. Frano was a super rugby union player and he is one of those converts who had such natural gifts that his transition to rugby league was a triumph. We battled away to be first-choice first five-eighths in the year after the Cavaliers' return, but given the rub of the green through his selection in the "Baby Blacks" who played that stimulating match against France after the banning of the Cavaliers, he performed so well he locked me out of the following series against the Wallabies.

Frano was gifted in the same way Steve Pokere was gifted with all those instinctive skills, great on his feet, good hands and he could run like a rabbit. Early on he lacked a rounded tactical feel for the game, not always spot-on with options, but at the end of it he was a complete player and a fine goal-kicker. We kept each other honest, our competition fierce but healthy, good for both of us.

Frano was the choice of the selectors in France in 1986 though it became a no-contest late in the tour when I suffered a severe injury at Bayonne. Strange to-do about that injury. I took a couple

Frano Botica, a super player – we kept each other honest.

An occasion of moment in 1985. With parents Ian and Pam Fox, left, and Merv and Yvonne Wallace, right.   photo, Fulton Photography

A rare event, a family together at home.

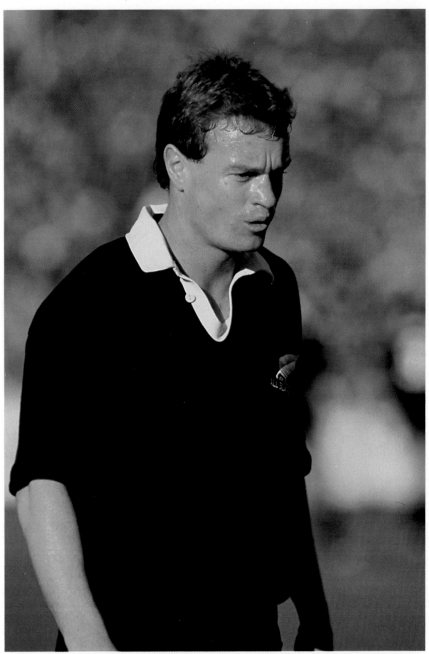

Deep breathing, hand-shaking, relaxing, concentrating and keeping the crowd waiting. Kicking for goal against France, second test, 1989.

of heavy knocks about the ribs and was uncomfortable after the game. The team doctor thought it could be displaced vertebrae and I had manipulation to restore them. During preparations for the test at Toulouse there were gurgling sensations in the right side of my chest. I was still tender, saw the doctor, he diagnosed my neck to be at fault and gave me some injections.

I trained in the lead-up to the test at Toulouse and in the match sat on the bench to watch Frano Botica do his stuff. I felt decidedly off-colour at halftime and by the end of the game I knew something was seriously wrong but I could not persuade the doctor I needed to get back to our hotel quickly. In fact, I got a point-blank refusal both at the after-match function and at the mayoral reception which followed. Then the room spun and I went down. I couldn't stand. Marty Berry and JK took me outside to wait for the ambulance. When I tried to sit up I blacked out. At the hospital they found a broken rib which had healed over, the pleural cavity full of blood and the right lung collapsed. They anaesthetised the area, put a needle in and whipped away 300mls of blood. During the next few days they took a total of half a litre, a proportion of which was probably red wine of no great distinction, for at the hospital they served it with breakfast, lunch and dinner. The broken rib I put down to a Steve Pokere tackle at Wellington earlier in the season, a real cruncher which gave me hell later on but which showed nothing on x-ray.

It did my condition no good at all to watch France beat the All Blacks 16-3 at Nantes, an occasion which squatted like an ogre in the All Blacks' psyche till they exorcised it in the World Cup final. Brian Lochore took that team to France intent on restoring unity of spirit in the All Blacks, for the signs of fragmentation were unmistakable following the Cavaliers' banning then their return to All Black status. In spite of the defeat at Nantes – or, in some ways, because of it – he achieved that and it was a notable factor in the way the team came together in 1987.

By the late '80s Frano was a highly polished player but by then I had established myself in the All Blacks through the World Cup and it is damned hard to get out of a successful team. It might be argued Frano had more strings to his bow than I. Assuredly he was a better runner and he was a very positive support player. After he went to league I found motivation had lost the razor-edge his presence brought to it. I did not feel as threatened. Frano and I brought out the best in each other and it was my good fortune that when the numbers went up for the World Cup of 1987 mine was number 10.

It may have been significant to my selection that John Hart and Grizz Wyllie had come into the All Black selection panel, Colin Meads having been given the elbow for his part in the

Cavaliers tour, a penalty which saddened the players to whom he had shown intense loyalty.

That year I felt for the first time a New Zealand selection panel sat down and worked out a style of game to beat specific opponents. They identified Australia and France as the World Cup teams most likely to trouble the All Blacks. On that assessment they picked a team to play the style of rugby to win. In the past I am sure selectors had picked their best 15 players and then set down the style they wanted them to play. That was doing things backward. In terms of pure individual ability it could be argued that three or four players were desperately unlucky to miss out on the World Cup. But the selectors went for players with the skill factors which matched the playing patterns they had designated. This approach was crucial to the events which followed.

Another vital factor was that the New Zealand Rugby Union, as a result of a heady adventure into enlightened thinking, brought in fitness scientist Jim Blair who had honed to fitness Auckland and Canterbury teams for seasons. He was able to take each player and design a programme which would bring him to a peak at the right time, his training schedule individualised to the finest degree. He insinuated skillwork and teamwork into physical training. Nothing was a bore. It was designer-fitness and when the chips were down it was the quality of our physical condition as much as our tactics which took us beyond the pack.

A significant pointer to the impact New Zealand would have in the World Cup came in the trial at Whangarei where a shadow test XV swamped its opposition 41-10. By any standards the losing team was strong, including ten players who were or would become established All Blacks. The shadow team captain, Andy Dalton, suffered criticism for continually pointing to the posts for penalty kicks when the game was clearly won. It was to my advantage that he did. I was marking Frano and had to make every post a winner. Andy justified his decisions by making the very point that it was a trial and that he was obliged to give me every opportunity to stake a claim. I kicked five penalty goals and a couple of conversions. There were other pointers. Michael Jones was a knock-out in a loose forward trio that had everything the game plan demanded. Buck Shelford, Alan Whetton and Michael were dynamite. The grunters and grinders in the front were irresistible. Stevie McDowell, John Drake and Andy Dalton were a formidable power-pack, though when it came to the event Andy, troubled by a niggling hamstring, was to give way to Sean Fitzpatrick who by then was an explosive all-rounder, as mobile as a loose forward and as strong as a prop. They were qualities that fitted the All Black game-plan like a glove.

However, a key ingredient was the selection of John Gallagher

Kipper Gallagher – a key ingredient.

as fullback, a fleet, physical runner whose presence supplied the All Blacks with options unlimited. When Gallagher eventually converted to English rugby league the All Blacks suffered withdrawal symptoms. The missing link was not restored – could not be restored – and when we went to Britain, Ireland and France to win the Cup again, we had become predictable without him, our attacking options blunted.

With Gallagher the All Blacks had a superbly balanced side based, as any good side must be, on a tight five who were stolid in set pieces and extraordinarily mobile in field play. We had in David Kirk a versatile, thinking half-back with a good kicking game, a superior running game on the blind, an option-chooser almost by instinct. Warwick Taylor at second five-eighths was the 110 per cent man. I have never seen a player so unreservedly lay himself on the line for the All Blacks. Whether tackling, distributing, placing immense pressure on kicks or creating space by reaching through the tackle to pass he was the rugby player's rugby player and it was not until his retirement that the public outside Canterbury truly understood what he meant to the All Blacks.

Leading from the front – Captain Kirk in at the corner in the World Cup final against France. John Kirwan and Patrice Lagisquet are on hand for entirely different reasons.

Joe Stanley was the power-plant at centre. But more, Joe had such vision, such capacity to think ahead of the play, such control of his possession, such confidence in his control that whether it was in orthodox distribution or whether absorbing two tackles to create space and then setting the ball up, the team had the chance to capitalise.

In the 1987 World Cup John Kirwan was at his most devastating. He was the detonator of so many All Black assaults, whether thigh-bursting his way through tackles, fending like a jack-hammer or setting us up with those bursts around to the open which sucked in defenders.

And on the other wing Craig Green, the consummate pro, with that uncanny ability to gain space by subtle selection of lines and angles.

We had four options for running targets, we had presentation-quality second-phase ball and with the injection of Kipper Gallagher's speed we were able to keep defences guessing – whether he was thrusting in as a decoy, whether he was targeted to split the defence. Whatever it happened to be he was committing the opposition to worry about him.

Playing at first five-eighths was almost a self-indulgence, picking options while reclining on the cushion thrown down for me by the forwards. Fly-half euphoria. Such was the time and space that even if I called a wrong move we could escape with it. And we were winning well while playing with such style that everyone seemed happy...well, other than some of the British media who watched our final against France with a jaundiced eye and suggested to David Kirk it had not been worthy of the occasion. Kirky, the man ever ready with the bon mot, was caught on the hop and responded very testily indeed. It was still in his eyes when he came back to the dressing-room. Disbelief.

During the World Cup Brian Lochore, an active, convincing coach himself, used Hart and Wyllie cleverly. The pair bounced off each other like yo-yos, amicable, humorous but deeply involved. Going into the quarter-final against Scotland there was concern over the strength of the Scottish front row and especially of Iain Milne who would be propping against Steve McDowell. McDowell was playing so well that probably nothing was beyond him but there was intense concentration on his technique for the Scotland match.

For the build-up Lochore threw the forwards to Wyllie, which was a bit like throwing them to the crocodiles. Crocodile Wyllie took them out for one session and put down about 80 scrums. Aucklanders were dropping like flies, which seemed to give Grizz a certain grim satisfaction. With Andy Dalton, an old foe of

The Club celebrates – Steve McDowell, Sean Fitzpatrick and John Drake with the World Cup.

A masterstroke – Brian Lochore, centre, pulled Grizz Wyllie and John Hart into an effective working partnership for the World Cup of 1987.

Milne, advising Steve the forwards scrummed for hours and at the end of it they knew to the last millilitre of blue-and-white sweat that nothing Scotland could do to them could surpass this. But at the end of it they also knew that technically the scrum was a machine.

The backs slogged away using the tackle-bags as opposition in setting up ball for second-phase action. The first time I hit the bag, I rode up it and the forwards were into me like a herd of rhino as I tried to present the ball. Alan Whetton got across me and whispered, "Lower, Foxy, lower, or you'll lose your bloody head." Great advice.

The Scottish game was our best of the World Cup tournament. I lived in dread of it. Dire, dire, dread. You lose a quarter-final you go home. I did not want to go home. Short of losing my bloody head to the All Black forwards, going home was what I least wanted to do. In the match everything came together, the perfect preparation for the semi-final and final. The Scots, great fighting opponents, were stunned by the power of the All Black pack.

I speak of that quarter-final rather than the semi-final against Wales or the final against France because it epitomised in the build-up and the match performance the character of New Zealand rugby as it was to take the next three years by storm. It was a brand of rugby which was to carry the All Blacks into perhaps the greatest era in New Zealand rugby history, the greatest not in the manner of odious comparison with the '20s or '60s, nor in player-comparison with the great ones of other eras, but the greatest in domination of world rugby and in the international kudos which bounced off it for New Zealand.

As a wry post-script to 1987 I think of a super photograph published after the final. It is of a laughing Grizz Wyllie and an uproarious John Hart, arms around shoulders, holding the trophy, their vision of the future uncluttered by dissidence or discord.

5

The years between

*Spin, spin, spin. Tackle, tackle, tackle. Spin it again, Foxy. Attack, attack,
attack. Move it wide, Foxy, move it wide, the buggers will break. Which
buggers? Horan and Little? Impregnable. Yes, JK! Go! Support! For
Christ's sake, where's the support? Some of it has a hammy. Some of it has
another hammy. Some of it has aggravated an injury about the sweaty area
known as the groin. Some of it hasn't had the rugby to cope with the
sustained pace. The bloody Aussies are sitting pretty on their lead. They're
challenging us to break them...13-6 doesn't break them. It breaks us.
Show's end, chaps, show's end...*

They'd been great years, the years between. Not years without conflict and not years, latterly, without defeat, but years
of such rugby that the All Blacks were saddled with un-
qualified greatness. That's always a sweet pill to swallow and a
bitter one to sick-up when the time comes. But the rugby made
the players feel great, too. Some of it was spin-off from the 1987
World Cup euphoria but much of it was the feeling kindled
within the team that we were a team of consequence. Team spirit
soared. Cynics might say that this is not uncommon among teams
which are winning. But it was more than the winning. It was the
way we were playing the game. It was as if, having settled to the
way we wanted to play, we could do anything within that
framework effectively while still having the style to spread
beyond it. And, given the occasion of a tight 60 minutes, we had
a built-in cushion of superior fitness which enabled us to stoke
our boiler in the last 20 minutes when the opposition flame was
flickering.

Heady years. Vintage Krug.

The '87 tour of Japan could not be shrugged off as too

superficial to be part of it...94-0, 74-0, 96-3, 106-4, 38-9, but beyond the huge scores, that tour under the coaching of John Hart and assistant Alex Wyllie and under the new captaincy of Buck Shelford cemented in place what the World Cup had achieved. It had much to do with the Japanese themselves. Rugby is not the national game but it is followed with fanaticism by its faithful thousands. The Japanese are among the most receptive crowds in the world, still essentially behind the Japanese players but almost embarrassingly generous in their acclaim for a visiting team they consider their guests.

I hope that olde-worlde notion never dies. It has done in some other countries where a visiting rugby team is an enemy off the field as well as on. Coming immediately to mind is Wales, where New Zealand teams in more recent years have had to suffer insult and aggro at times.

Perhaps at the bottom of it for the Welsh is loss of pride, loss of a team to be proud of.

Old All Blacks speak with great warmth of the Welsh behind the Welsh, the Welsh behind the angry crowds who abuse and revile touring teams. In their experience there is something of schizophrenia in Welsh rugby. They say that what one half of a Welshman does to you and says to you while you are out on the field playing his teams is far more than balanced by what the other half of him does for you when you meet him in the club, join him in his singing, share his jug and talk unremittingly of rugby. They say his love of rugby goes beyond even his patriotism for Wales.

I believe it all. I hope those days return. Those of us who have played in Wales more recently have experienced a different Welsh rugby supporter, one who knows little respect for common courtesies and who has no feeling whatever for the camaraderie you might expect the long history of Welsh-New Zealand rugby to have inspired and I believe still does among the players. I have known spitting from the Latins. I never expected to find in in Wales. I have been sworn at in New Zealand but I will not easily forget the obscenities which chundered out of Welsh supporters' mouths as I prepared to kick for goal. The All Blacks do not expect adulation. They do hope for some respect while expecting the ultimate in nationalistic barracking when they play abroad.

These feelings are shared by my team-mates, some of whom have experienced the physical backlash of having beaten a Welsh side. The Frightful Foyer Fracas at Llanelli in 1989 was a case in point. Two hard-case brothers decided to try out Joe Stanley and Andy Earl. It was, evidently, quite a show, too. But while the recriminations flew against our guys, investigation showed they

Jonathon Davies – his advice spurned by the Welsh. Result: Jonathon Davies, rugby league star.

were not at fault other than in the retaliation stakes. No charges were laid but had the worst come to the worst it was the intention of the touring party to front up and each claim 1/35th of the blame. But even before that there had been shows of animosity on the streets.

We had played Wales in New Zealand in 1988 for two huge wins but not achieved, especially in the second test, without being given a hint of what Welsh rugby could be if only it would get its act together, if only the leaping spirit of the players when they play for their clubs could be transmitted through the national team. It was in that second test that I had one of those rare days, a 100 per cent strike rate from 10 kicks – and got within spitting distance of my first try in test rugby before Jonathon Davies buried me.

Jonathon had so much to give to rugby union and was deeply committed to giving it. When the Welsh team went home he sought to convey to the Welsh Rugby Union what had been learned in New Zealand and to encourage the administration to

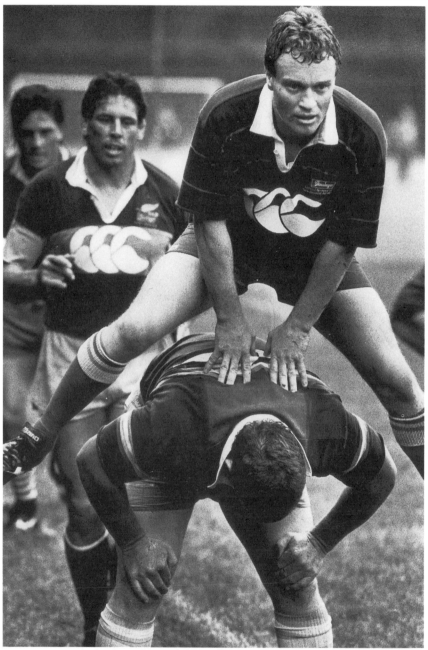

We train for the Welsh on the tour of 1989. Leapfrog was the closest it came to fun.

take that learning and convert it into a campaign to lift Welsh rugby out of the mire. He was rejected like a peasant. Here he was, Wales' finest player by the length of the Taff and with the stature among the players of the game at all levels to be heard and heeded. The rejection cut deeply into his soul and I have no doubt that was the real beginning of his rugby league career.

The attitude of touring players to their treatment in Wales so concerned New Zealand rugby's own happy Welshman, Phil Kingsley-Jones, the Counties coaching co-ordinator, that in 1991 he rounded up Pinetree Meads, John Sturgeon, Ian Jones, Terry Wright and myself and took us to his old club, Nantyglo. There I saw the side of Welsh rugby the old-timers speak of with such enthusiasm and affection. We had a ball. One little guy fronted up to me, looked over his shoulder with an air of deep conspiracy and said, "What do you call a Welshman in the World Cup final?" What could I say without being too objectionable, though I knew the answer had to be some sort of insult. He answered himself, "The referee" and rocked with laughter, infecting us with it, as much tickled by the shock-factor of a Welshman taking the mickey out of himself and the current state of Welsh rugby for the entertainment of New Zealanders as by the joke itself. In the circumstances it was difficult to know how hard to laugh. Appreciation of a good Welsh joke is one thing, making a meal of that particular joke in a Welsh rugby club another and not in the best interests of Welsh-Kiwi accord. So I hid my face in another jug. If only we, as a team, could have experienced that sort of night on the 1989 tour it would have done much for mutual goodwill. As it was, it was sad, sad, sad. We couldn't get out of Wales quickly enough but the animosity had been such that we felt the Welsh might have been saying good riddance anyway. Old Welsh players with whom old New Zealand players feel such affinity will recoil from that judgement. I wish it did not have to be made. The history of rugby between the two countries is so rich, an adventure storybook of heroes and the respect of the heroes of one side for those of the other. That the relationship has soured to the point where New Zealand players are made to feel like invaders rather than welcome guests is a blow to rugby itself.

But having said all these things, for they fairly reflect the temper of New Zealand players, I am reminded that I sat in the stand for the game against Neath, the club they call the Welsh All Blacks. The day had started without high promise of a smooth ride. The All Blacks had arrived to find their dressing-room locked and not a key this side of the border. With only 30 minutes to go before kick-off Grizz Wyllie's eyebrows were down around his nostrils. He'd had enough. He sized the door up, twitched his left shoulder twice and the door went quietly. A polished performance, roundly applauded. It was a tough game. All around me was bloody bedlam. Meek filing clerks from the office, their docile hymn-loving wives and their boy-soprano kids were transformed into screaming, demented nutters. I could not believe the lashings of abuse. It was stuff from another world. The guy in front of me was raving. Quite nuts. He screamed abuse without control, so bad that in a passing moment of remorse one of the other Neath supporters whacked him with his umbrella. It brought a moment's resentful silence. Then he was away again, uncontrollable. The final whistle went. He rolled up his abuse tongue, inserted a replacement, turned to me, smiled like a saint, shook hands, said quietly, "Jolly good game boys" and went home to feed his pigeons.

That chap might very well have been everything about Welsh rugby we did not understand and did not have the opportunity to get to know better in front of a blazing log fire with a jug of ale in the clubhouse.

Throughout the Welsh segment of the tour the irresistible message was that the players were better players for their clubs than for Wales.

Collectively, they found fire in their bellies and something approaching hostility in their hearts when they put on the colours of their clubs and went out in front of their fans. Paul Thorburn, the Welsh captain, denied club spirit was higher than the spirit of Wales but it was difficult to come to any other conclusion. At Newport the players turned their backs on the haka and had they set out deliberately to rouse Buck Shelford they could not have done it better. Buck said, "Right. We'll take it to them," and the haka line, led by a fired-up Buck, bore down on the Newport players. Originally, our haka was not meant to intimidate. As always, as we see it, it was a traditional challenge, a challenge to play rugby. But in this case intimidation was close to everyone's heart.

I hope Welsh rugby does not sink deeper into its sea of troubles. With the pillaging of its players by rugby league, with its apparent reluctance to accept help, with its shallow consideration of schools rugby, with the indifference at the top level to the game's basic skills, it seems hellbent off-course. No one wants that. Better by far for all of rugby to have a rampant Wales. It would be a tragedy of the game were the Welsh administration to turn in on itself and lock out enlightenment in the rebuilding of its game.

After Wales, the flight to Ireland was a flight in more ways than one. It was that in more ways than two for Mike Brewer who met a stewardess named Beverley, to become Mrs Brewer. It was, as the Mills and Boon sexpots say, a felicitous omen for what was

Irish eyes were not smiling when the skipper, Willie Anderson, eyeballed the All Black haka. But the tour was an all-round delight.

to become a wonderful tour.

The Irish take their rugby very seriously. Like their Guinness. And like their poteen on those rare occasions when they are able to blarney the little people into letting them have a drop. But when the game is done the Irish let go of it without recrimination. They can laugh at themselves more readily than any other people I have met and they can make you laugh at yourself without restraint.

There was one unpleasant event among dozens of sheer delight. The Irish, inspired by their captain, Willie Anderson, forced a bizarre confrontation before the test when they chested up to the All Blacks during the haka and tried to shout us down. Steve McDowell, proudly a Maori, swore that if one Irishman had touched him at that time, it would have been the shortest test in history for both of them. The Irish, being what they are, would have taken Stevie to their hearts and created a legend in song and story about the All Black who was ordered off before the game began.

Just as the Welsh were, all the Irish teams were desperate to do well against us but were not able, or did not plan, to create positive movement themselves. So their rugby lacked smooth control. Basically, they sought to disrupt our game patterns. It was physically testing without being exhausting. Contact was not in the same hard, grafting manner which brings exhaustion after a close-fought match. It was a contact of elbows and knees and any other bones and angles which could be brought into play to knock us off balance.

For me, in an off beat way, Ireland was the most intimidating country of all, the crowds worse by far than the abusive Welsh. They were so bloody quiet when I kicked for goal! I was unnerved by it. They live by one of the game's finest graces: give the kicker a fair go. That happens so rarely these days – even, I might say, in New Zealand where once, long ago I am told, it was held to be a matter of pride to be quiet while the kicker had his time on stage. I have become so used to challenging the barrackers in my mind – the whistlers, the bloody buglers, the loony trombonists, the fireworks nuts and the boring, boring booers – to do their worst while I kick the goals that the silence of the Irish was like someone bashing cymbals against my head (and there's got to be something Irish about that).

As the kicker retires from the ball there's a great shushing around the ground. It sounds like a million Irish mums calming their babes. Then if someone dares break the code of silence the ground announcer waves his shillelagh and all is quiet. Magic.

In Ireland the boys shrugged off the depression of Wales, regained their humour. For Bernie McCahill, son of that famous Irish Kiwi, Barney, it was a journey into unadulterated delight, some sort of homecoming. A pint of Guinness, an Irishman to tell lies to and Bernie was in paradise. The feel of Ireland and the warmth of the people infected everyone with winter madness. On the journey out of Eire into Northern Ireland we stopped the bus for what in more elevated circles is known as a comfort stop but which, because we are notoriously unelevated, we call a pisso. As we lined up at the side of the road, adopting the age-old male posture, Kevin Schuler suddenly leapt the fence, barking like a demented collie-cross bitch. He ranged far and wide, running like a stag, rounding up a flock of thunderstruck Irish sheep while Richard Loe did the gentleman-farmer bit from the roadside, whistling, gesticulating, swearing, cajoling until Schuler had the sheep, quivering and resentful, in some sort of order. It was a superior Country Calendar performance and warmly applauded by a discerning gallery.

This act was marginally better than that of Joe Stanley who, in the meantime, had stolen the team bus, and that of the border police as we crossed into Northern Ireland. Sirens wailed, straight-faced threats were made and we were jail-meat "unless, if you wouldn't mind, sorr, signin' yer auto-graph for me little gorrl". Thank God for the fun of Ireland.

It was on that tour of Wales and Ireland that our last-quarter domination became almost a trademark. It may be that the occasions when we were pushed into making that final quarter count were an encouragement to those studying us from other countries that invincibility was, indeed, a myth and that last quarters can be made to count as effectively by a staunch, suffocating defence as by the need to attack and overcome for points. It may even be that Australians were especially taken with that theorem.

Bernie McCahill, a pint of Guinness, an Irishman to lie to and he was in heaven.

That tour plus a match in Canada brought the All Blacks 14 wins from 14 matches, 71 tries to 7 and in the two internationals 7 tries to none. As an indication of the depth of our kicking strength, John Gallagher kicked 5 penalty goals and 10 conversions, Frano Botica 8 penalty goals and 14 conversions and I 15 penalty goals and 19 conversions. And in the wings on that tour was a young man named Matthew Ridge, before long to become a kicking phenomenon for Manly in Australian rugby league. Gallagher, Botica, Ridge...all players of rich quality to be lost from rugby union. And on the departure of fullbacks Gallagher and Ridge hangs a tale of much consequence to the future performance of the All Blacks and the World Cup of 1991.

To fully appreciate the tale it is important to scan the statistics of the All Black tour of Australia in 1988. They show that from fullback Gallagher scored 12 tries, one more than the best wing in the world at that time, John Kirwan. That is not a comparison of the players but it does illustrate in the most graphic way how the All Blacks used a swift-striking fullback of immaculate timing in their grand plan. The All Blacks as a team were the key

Kevin (Sheepdog) Schuler impressed Irish players with this sort of charge and Irish sheep with his mustering technique.

opening up the door for Gallagher but, equally, Gallagher was the key to the attacking options the All Blacks luxuriated in. There is the starting point of a road which had its ending in Dublin in 1991 without Gallagher. And, of comparable point, without Ridge.

Before I travel that rocky road it is important to consider events which, on the field and off, made it rocky. I have said that Lansdowne Road, Dublin, 1991, brought the end of a great All Black era. Others may point to our defeat by Australia at Athletic Park, Wellington, in 1990, as the effective end of it because that was our first defeat after a run of 50 matches and 23 tests since 1986. But it was the third test of a series we won two tests to one. It may be argued that the Australians' 21-12 win in Sydney rather outweighed our 6-3 win in Auckland before the World Cup last year, but the Bledisloe Cup stayed in New Zealand. To my mind the real match-play championship was in Dublin for it was there on the world stage that the Wallabies snuffed out the All Black candle.

One of my occasional moments of silence. Sleeping it off in the Bullet Train, Japan, 1987.

Hob-nobbing at the Ellerslie races with Kieran Crowley and mutual friend Gary Freeman, who plays a different game altogether.

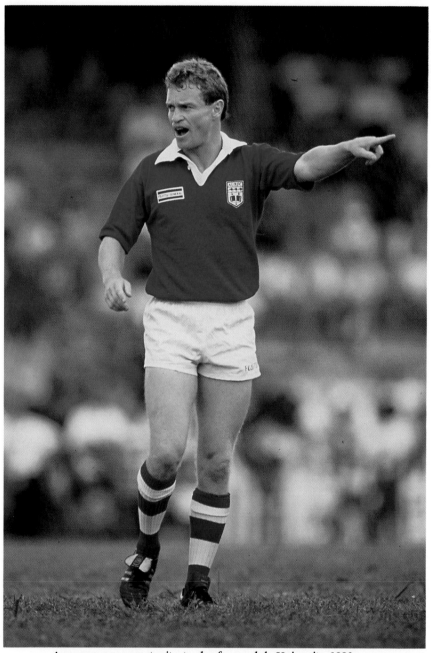

An uncommon opportunity to play for my club, University, 1990.

6

The fullback factor

So that's it then. The dressing room tells it all. It is the dressing-room of defeat. The silence of champagne corks not popping. The silence of no laughter. The silence of no clowns. Heads hang down between knees. Ian Jones has wet eyes. Grant Fox feels agonisingly sick. Alan Whetton is agonisingly sick. Grizz, Harty and Lane Penn tell us they know we have given our guts. AJ is still giving his. They're proud of us, they say. But the heads stay down. Andy Earl, gruff old Wurzel, tires of it. "Bugger this," he yells, "Get your heads up, you bastards, and have a beer." So, because Wurzel is pretty aggro about it, we do.

For me, emotionally, the next morning was worse. Getting on the plane to fly to Wales and Cardiff Arms while the Aussies lined up for the flight to England and Twickenham was as if someone without mercy or anaesthetic was twisting a knife somewhere around the aorta. It bloody-well hurt. Even though I might not have been fit to play at Twickenham, anyway, it still bloody-well hurt.

It hadn't been much of a night, either. I had played the match over and over. I had played it with the injury and I had played it without the injury. The frustrating thing was that I didn't play it any better and we still lost. Then there was that other thing. Should I have come off? At 13-0 down should I have conceded victory to my injury and come off? Should I have turned my back on a game that was getting away from us? Yes, you say? Should Bernie McCahill have come off with his hammy? Yes, you say? Should John Timu have submitted to his hammy? Yes, you say? Easy playing it out there in telly-land, eh? No contest out there. No self-debate out there whether you let your team down by staying or whether by going.

How do you walk away when your team is down? Much easier when your team is doing well, but even then I'm reluctant. So what did I think? I was concerned that if I went off in a match of this intensity I would be replaced by an inexperienced player. That was pretty stupid. Jon Preston is a fine player and very self-controlled. But in the heat of the contest it seemed a hell of a useful rationale for staying on.

So much in that game comes back to Campo. His try, his dream-pass to Horan for the other – and my bloody injury, Campo. Thirty minutes into the game and Campo is on the counter attack. I think I have him covered. A lot of players have thought they had Campo covered. Suddenly he jets to go around me. I turn with that swell of panic rising in the throat and I know I have to take off and turn my tackle into an ankle-tap. I'm on a long stride, straining to get to him when the groin tightens up like a vice. Thirteen-nil down, 50 minutes to play, Fox a passenger.

And what about that injury? How come I carried it out of Argentina, played the tests against Australia, came to the World Cup, played against Canada with a pain-killing injection for a strained quad muscle (a spin-off injury) and then had the thing go after 30 minutes of the semi-final? How come all that, while Mike Brewer couldn't pass his medical and had to stay at home and play staggeringly well for Otago? I don't know and I'm not about to second-guess a medical panel. It was said there was one rule for Mike and another for me. I can only say I recorded on my medical form what my injury was, I was tested rigorously and I was not troubled by it at that time.

It had started during a goal-kicking session in Argentina. I was just aware of what seemed to be a minor abdominal strain. Then, preparing for the first test, I bent to tie my laces and there was a brief burning sensation at the pubic bone. The day before the test I went to my usual kicking session and when I kicked for goal there was a tearing sensation. I tried for kick-offs and there was a fierce pain. Back at the hotel I could hardly walk.

I talked to Doc Mayhew. Lie down, he said. Easy. Sit up, he said. What? I said. Sit up, he said. And I couldn't. Lift your legs, he said. My legs? I said. And I couldn't. Doc shook his head and said, "Osteitis pubis." It sounded like some anti-social disease I'd caught off a public lavatory seat. Reassure me, Doc. No, no, nothing like that. It is an irritation of the pubic bone. Call it kickers' disease. Common in soccer, not unknown in rugger. Here, have an injection.

Kickers' disease? Let me explain. The pubic bone is in two pieces linked by cartilage. In my case the right side of the bone had become disconnected from the cartilage. That places a strain on the pelvis and just about everything else as one thing compensates for another and places pressure somewhere else, which...why the hell couldn't it have been the lavatory seat job?

I told Grizz and Gary Whetton there was a distinct possibility I wouldn't be able to play. The next morning it felt freer but I was still acutely aware of it. I gave myself a test on the grass outside the BA Sheraton. Passing Argentines glanced at me, raised their eyebrows, shrugged and displayed an unflattering lack of recognition. Running was painful but did not become worse than that. Kicking hurt but, with a jab, I could cope with that. In the match I felt no pain, like a night-out with Grizz, kicked 17 points and made an abysmal clearance blunder which gave Argentina one of their two tries. It is of some point here to note that critics of the New Zealand performance (we won 28-14) were concerned that Kieran Crowley lacked a yard or so of pace when we developed scoring opportunities from support play.

Doc Mayhew – a dab-hand with kickers' disease.

We pulled the strings together in the second test, which we won 36-6. My 20 points were taken at the expense of quite severe aggravation of the injury. The only cure, I was told, was rest. Difficult, that. I'm a hopeless rester. So I relied on treatment and modified training routines. Maybe I should have opted out of everything till the World Cup. Maybe I should have pulled out of everything including the World Cup until it was absolutely right. But the pull to play for Auckland, to round-off our World Cup preparation against the Aussies and the lure of the World Cup itself locked out all other consideration. I was not going to see four years of hard work going down the gurgler. I can understand how Mike Brewer felt.

When the team was picked for the Aussie series Grizz and the medical panel were aware that I was carrying what became nicely simplified as "a groin strain", which has been known to cover a multitude of sins and sinners. But near enough. The

Aussies beat us roundly, 21-12, at Sydney in what was the hardest match I have ever played against them, including the World Cup semi. They were playing so well and we not so well I was sure we were heading for a 20-point stuffing.

Here, they were always threatening where at Dublin in the semi-final, having established what they judged to be a commanding margin, they sat. In Sydney they kept the ball away from us and forced us into that humiliating situation of always seeming to be chasing. How could this be? We had sharpened ourselves for this. We were fizzing three days before it as if, beyond any game of rugby ever played anywhere, this was the one the guys had been waiting for. Three days before. There's the rub. On the day we played like jokers just in from a three-day hill-country muster. The nervous energy was left out in the hills. We could not set up targets for the forwards to run to. If you were to say Fox had an average game I'd have to call you a liar. A generous liar.

It is of more than passing interest that we had our swift, polished finisher, Terry Wright, at fullback and he played well. Planning ahead, it's called. Less succinctly, it is also called trying to replace John Gallagher when there is no Matthew Ridge because we are desperate to restore the options – or something approaching them – which made us unbeatable after the first World Cup. We recaptured some of our ego in the second of the home and away matches, this time at Auckland, when we took a much more stable hand in proceedings, conspired to lock up Michael Lynagh and throw away the key, established superiority in the lineouts and came through 6-3 winners. Indecently modest, you might judge. But satisfying, looking ahead to the likelihood of a World Cup semi-final.

Those matches against Australia were the second phase of a three-pronged plan for 1991. The first was Argentina and the third the World Cup. In our minds they hung together. We were the most successful team to tour Argentina since the 1976 All Blacks but, in hindsight, the tour was far too long for its purpose. We had nine games including two tests. We could have achieved our World Cup requirements in five games.

In bald logistics Argentina is not the easiest place to tour. T-bone steaks approximately the size of a leg of hogget are just fine but when they seem to make the most lasting impact from a whole rugby tour you have to wonder what we took from Argentina which was going to be valuable to us for the World Cup. The difficulty was that on this tour the Argentines never went out to play positive rugby against us. They went out to negate what we did, to work at not getting beaten by too many – and the way to do this was by a planned campaign of offside play. I have never experienced anything approaching it before or since. The Italians were pretty good at it in the World Cup, but if they wish to develop it further as an art-form they should call in the masters from the pampas.

As a World Cup build-up phase I would give the Argentina tour 6 out of 10 and two of the six would be for the steaks.

We came back and went into the Australian games. The Aussies had spent three years preparing for the World Cup. As with other teams, they used the years between experimentally, building, stitching into their fabric new players, siphoning the essence of the All Blacks' success from the experience of 1987. New Zealand had been astonishingly open-handed with the secrets of its training and fitness techniques. If some responsible person were to call us mugs I don't know that I could muster up a constructive argument against it.

Through those years international teams meeting defeat were able without recrimination to relate their defeats to their World Cup build-up. The All Blacks, always under unremitting demand to win from their public, their critics and themselves, would concede a defeat at their peril. In all the games we played during the late '80s and into the '90s the Australians and the Scots were the only teams prepared to attack us rather than stop us. The Scots of 1990 detected that within our new team framework there was a less positive line of communication and a less coherent defensive system. They came desperately close to us in the second test when they scored two tries to one in a 21-18 defeat.

The first test had brought me my first try in test rugby. I would like to be able to record that I brilliantly scooped up a bad pass, zipped, zapped, dummied and feinted to beat the whole Scottish team one by one before making a final 30-metre sprint to score under the posts as the crowd went wild. But I can't. I'm not really your zipper and zapper nor your 30-metre sprinter. I can say I started the action by sloping an angled kick to space where Iwan Tukalo botched a fly-kick clearance and I was there again to score the try. Quite unlike my try against Ireland at Dublin the previous year...Fox goes wide, half a dummy, around the remnants of the defence and over. Great try, Foxy. Now kick the conversion. Dream on. As I placed the ball the ballboy from the opposite side of the field ran over and told the referee, Sandy MacNeill, that his touch-judge had had his flag out for a long, long time. Jim Fleming, of Scotland, had flagged Sean Fitzpatrick at a lineout for stepping into the field of play when throwing in. I guess you could say it's so common and so ignored by touch-judges that it is almost a hooker's prerogative to step over the line as he throws. At a time when the game is committed to abolish pedantry in refereeing and to bring alertness and understanding

Brilliant, Foxy, just brilliant. Now forget it. The non-try against Ireland, 1989.

to such seriously neglected matters as the advantage law, Jim's flag on Sean was what you could fairly call Victorian primness. Buck Shelford told a reporter I used unprintable language. Apart from the fact that no language seems too extreme to be printable these days, what I said was absolutely nothing. Not aloud. Afterward Sean and I talked with Jim Fleming over an ale, a pleasant exchange of viewpoint with no ill-will at all.

Coming through the season before the World Cup we still had players from 1987. From the pack we had lost some of the great warriors of that campaign, prop John Drake, lock Murray Pierce and Buck Shelford. Big Murray had gone to South Africa to have a season with Natal but found his size weighed heavily against him. Too small. Big enough to hold together a World Cup winning scrum but too small for Natal. There's an omen there. David Kirk was getting some academic posh at Oxford University and would be a television comments man for the cup tournament. Second five-eighths Warwick Taylor, wing Craig Green and the ill-fated appointed captain of 1987, Andy Dalton, had gone through the attrition mill. Joe Stanley was to come to France with us, but was not to play in the tests. I believe not taking Smokin' Joe to the World Cup was a serious fault in selection. As a team we missed those comprehensive qualities he brought to our midfield. Joe came to test rugby at the age of 29 and just kept

Smokin' Joe at full smoke – he should have been at the World Cup.

getting better. Craig Innes was an improver; Joe was still the best and we missed him.

Following Warwick's departure John Schuster slotted into the backline superbly between myself and Joe. There was something uncanny about the instinctive mind-to-mind play of Schuster and his devastating Wellington buddy Gallagher, running in from fullback. With Joe such a physical and mentally-deft force at centre we had it good, so very good. Buck Shelford had become an inspirational captain, his performance on the Wales-Ireland tour of 1989 awesome, his captaincy resting securely on an apparently limitless capacity to lead from the front, to inspire by example. The most damaging blow to our World Cup aspirations was not, however, the demise of Buck as captain after the tests against Scotland in 1990. No matter the prolonged public outrage over Buck's dismissal, events preceding it were of greater consequence to the campaign. The loss of Kipper Gallagher to rugby league was critical. The almost-simultaneous loss of Matthew Ridge to league was devastating.

Matthew had become heir-apparent to Kipper. He had toured in Ireland and Wales and his rugby union future was clearcut and exciting. He had come through the Auckland nursery, first as a brash, arrogant kid then, under the down-to-earth tutelage of Professor Joe Stanley, as a good team-man, gutsy as all get-out, aggressive at times to the point of belligerence, skilled but still with the arrogance to him that makes some otherwise merely good rugby players outstanding. He did not have Kipper's burning speed but he was fast enough and, like Kipper, he had a physical run which, blasting through the middle, placed strenuous demands on a defence. He was a superb defensive fullback – better defensively than Kipper, better in the air and he could kick well. He was heir-apparent in every way.

I am confident Matthew would not have gone to Manly had he known Kipper was negotiating with Leeds. He had a fierce ambition to play test rugby and I think he would have stayed around at least for the World Cup and then, maybe, gone to league. For union and the All Blacks it was sad neither knew the other's plans. Sad? Read that tragic.

Then we lost Johnny the Schu, the man with the magic feet, who knew my play and absorbed the vocal velocity of my game so well, the ideal man in the middle with his twinship understanding with Kipper and a linkage with Joe which exploited the centre's vision and brilliant distribution skills. Gallagher gone, Ridge gone, Schuster gone. Not only, but most importantly, a brake on our attacking range but a disturbance to our defensive organisation.

The event and the aftermath of The Dropping of Buck will find

Matthew Ridge – Gallagher's loss was critical, Ridge's devastating.

Johnny the Schu – mind-to-mind contact with Gallagher uncanny.

their place in another context because they were to be the fuse to a powder-keg of allegations and rumour, maliciously inspired, of which I was a target and which placed their own special sort of pressure on the players. Suffice to say at this point that I was surprised when Buck was dropped and that what happened to Buck was between him and the selectors. I was also surprised he did not more swiftly volunteer some facts to dispel damaging rumours of player-conspiracy against him and of physical dressing-room confrontation after the second test against Scotland. The public attitude to the All Blacks from that point was coloured by the belief in the age-old fiction that where there is smoke there has to be fire. Willingness to believe that has been at the root of many of man's injustices to man and at the heart of character-assassination by rumour. Regrettably, it is a belief which has a firm grip on the New Zealand psyche. It is the beginning of the great clobbering machine, the Kiwi version of the tall poppy syndrome.

Kieran Crowley came into the team for Gallagher and Walter Little for Schuster. Craig Innes, who had played robustly and with success on the wing in Wales and Ireland, came in to centre when Joe, with that chronic chest complaint and being judged to have lost a yard of pace, was not selected for the tests against Australia at home and against France over there.

Public and media were all-forgiving when, with Gary Whetton appointed captain and Zinny Brooke number eight, the All Blacks had a win of great quality over the Wallabies in the first test, were less elated with a 10-point win in the second and positively outraged when the Aussies gave us our first beating in 24 tests at Athletic Park – the match in which, having scored the only try, Phil Kearns, the Australian hooker, gave Sean Fitzpatrick the most pugnacious invitation to a barby ever delivered on a rugby field. Phil's violent two-finger erection was no more than a kindly suggestion to Fitzy that he could even have two sausages.

Two losses in the programme before the first test of the French tour which followed brought criticism of the team, of individuals, of selectors to fever-pitch. We deserved to be criticised. Any group of players who achieve such a level of performance that they represent their country deserve and should expect criticism when they do not perform at that level. That's a simple fact of sporting life. In my experience acute sensitivity to criticism comes when there is desertion from fair analysis, whether through ignorance or design, and when the desire to cut down individuals at any cost becomes paramount. The trend toward tabloid sensationalism is unmistakable, not only in print but in television as well. Constructive criticism can be aggressive criticism, but gratuitous sensationalism at the expense of individuals is in another league.

Some of the criticism from France went beyond what even the players had come to expect. Some of it was so persistent it smacked of criticism with some motive other than legitimate comment. It created a distinctly abrasive relationship between media and players. It eventuated that after the losses to Provence-Cote D'Azur and Cote Basque the New Zealand television commentator Keith Quinn, essentially a fair man, had been instructed from his New Zealand headquarters to get stuck into us as a matter of policy.

For the players, at least, our overwhelming victories in the two tests were sweet. That the All Blacks could go back to Nantes, scene of their 1986 downfall, and outplay France so comprehensively after a build-up which was less than satisfactory was a highlight in the careers of some players. Pre-match tension was heavy. Every player felt it. Although I had not been involved in the 1986 match I wanted to win this one because of it. The 24-3 scoreline was impressive. It might have been 6-3 and still been exhilarating because of the history of Nantes.

The French are rugby's sublime schizophrenics, passionate, emotive, dirty, gallant, cynical, brilliant, abysmal, elated, sad, innovative, mad. Their administration connives to frustrate touring teams, their forwards connive to mangle and maim, their liaison officers refuse to speak English. But for all that, it's a great place to tour.

Before Nantes, test newcomers to France were warned. Eye-gouging, head-butting, kicking and bollock-scrambling – expect them all and don't let them get away with it. The French forwards were, I must say, meticulous in fulfilling those expectations. One prop, Seigne, was an outright bloody nuisance and late in the game, off-camera, out of mind, he went off to bye-byes. Very stylish, we thought, very French to just drop off like that during a test match. He did, however, appear to be nursing a nose, an oddly misshapen one. The fair presumption was that it had happened in the dressing-room before the game when the French props were doing their one-on-one butting practice. The nearest All Black did seem to be Stevie McDowell but it couldn't have been him. He was wearing an angelic half-smile that said, "This baby is innocent". Stevie and I have been through a lot together. We played our colts' rugby together and we played our first test together in Argentina. He was, without doubt, the best loosehead prop in the world before the World Cup and, in spite of some extraordinary assessments to the contrary, he was still the best loosehead prop in the world after it. He is a man who honours the rule that you always give the referee a bit of time to sort out a problem. He is patient but not biblically so. He never hit a guy who didn't deserve it and Seigne sure deserved it - not that one presupposes the other, of course.

It has been said by many players that the French are the most difficult players to plan for, that their unpredictability requires some sort of matching unpredictability, that they never know when they are beaten and that when they are down they are at their most dangerous. My own feeling is that the French have become one of the easiest of all to plan for. One simple game plan: command possession, construct moves close to the set piece, turn them around, bomb them, and just occasionally go wide.

Stevie McDowell – the best loosehead prop before the World Cup and after it.

The French are good scrummagers but they are not great lineout players and in second phase play they lack cohesion. They do tend to leave holes close to the set piece because of their obsession with cutting off wide options. Accurate up-and-unders are an effective offensive weapon and the French, especially, do not handle them well. In 1989 in the Lancaster Park test we scored from a bomb when John Schuster was there to bang Serge Blanco and Alan Whetton gobbled up the try. Any team which does not commit itself to the tackle deserves to lose to the French because they love to have you on one on one. You might base any game on the pattern I suggest but against the French, and the Fijians, too, it is especially effective.

The French tryline is not easy to get to but the goalposts are. Their indiscipline brings penalties and these days most teams have top goalkickers. If the French were able to rein-in their tempers they would be more consistently formidable.

Napoleon Jacques Fouroux – took the French out of French rugby.

Jacques Fouroux tried to distort French rugby so that it became something else. He would, he said, manufacture a continental All Blacks. But his insistence that he was copying the All Blacks was ill-based and the concept ill-advised. He did not understand the subtleties of what we were doing, failed to perceive the nuances of ball distribution through players like Schuster and Stanley and their ability to put Gallagher into space at speed. Yet that wide passage of attack through the extra runner had once been, almost by tradition, a huge French strength. He simplified everything to big is beautiful, which took no account of big also being mobile and big being big in heart and big in discipline.

Philippe Sella – his genius suffocated by Fouroux's All Black phobia.

So Fouroux squeezed out of French rugby much of "French rugby" and it was a staggering administrative blunder that he was allowed to do it for so long. There were players of such rare brilliance, such vision – Blanco, Sella, Lafond, Mesnel – who could turn a losing game around with sheer free-flow magic, but too often they were servants of a madly restrictive policy.

It should not be assumed that because the team under Gary Whetton had so decisively won the tests in France all at home was forgiven or forgotten. The rumour-machine babbled on through the summer.

There was something approaching campaign status against us when we were in Argentina last year. The man who suffered most severely from this was Grizz Wyllie, whose coaching came under orchestrated attack, inspired by one man's conviction that John Hart should be the All Black coach. There was deep resentment in the team that as recent an All Black as Andy Haden should stage-manage television to that end. Knowing Andy for the astute man he is, I would have thought he would perceive that a campaign of this sort could have only one end: a rebound against Hart.

That there was still no Buck rankled deeply and the Bring Back Buck campaign became a cult-assault on Gary Whetton but its related victims were Zinny Brooke, Buck's replacement, and the team generally. What hit the players, and I am sure Grizz, was that old All Blacks were so ready to weigh in with criticisms of individuals, something which went on and on through the World Cup and the recriminations which followed. There is something pathetic about old players who were so sensitive to criticism themselves, especially from critics at home on the other side of the world, virtually queuing-up to have their whack whether through television, radio or print.

When you become an international sportsman you accept you are vulnerable to public judgement, that you have critics who know the game and critics who do not, critics who skim like shags across the shallows of match analysis and personal performances, critics – and I believe with regret they are a dwindling number – who are sufficiently professional to research the game, learn from training runs what teams are trying to achieve and relate that to the match situation.

You accept you are not only playing for your team but for a public of diverse tempers one of which is resentment of the players when the reflected glory is taken from it by defeat.

It is the way of the world. For a decade the All Blacks gave New Zealand a feast. They were a winning team and in that climate few of them could do any wrong. Hero-worship was the order of the day and reflected glory was alive and kicking. Then there came close calls to Scotland, losses to Australia. Mistakes uncharacteristic of All Black rugby were made. The mood changed. Personalities were slagged-off. Rumour flew high, wide and ugly and like most rumour it was long on imagination and short on fact.

You put other things on the scales: that out there is also a public which loves rugby for the game, which feels for the players and their welfare, which is able to absorb less successful times without taking an aggro anti-player stance.

At the end of the day you play rugby because you enjoy it, for what it gives you in satisfaction, physical and mental, and for what playing it well does for the country. Rugby is a national barometer. Success is its high. The players do take pride in keeping the temperature hot. When it dips no one, and certainly not the game's fine-weather friends, feel it as strongly as the players. It is inevitable given the demands of modern rugby schedules that optimum performance will not, cannot, be sustained in match after match whether at provincial or international level and the players owe no apology for that. We are, however, under an obligation to the game, to the public and to ourselves to do more than go through the motions to achieve a win. We have to accept that if rugby is to progress it must be entertaining to watch, but not in some flighty way at the expense of the game's essential character. It has also far to go in adventurous, imaginative marketing of itself.

Blending individual skills into team performance is one of the game's big challenges and team performance at a superior level is the greatest satisfaction of all. It would be a serious miscalculation of what the

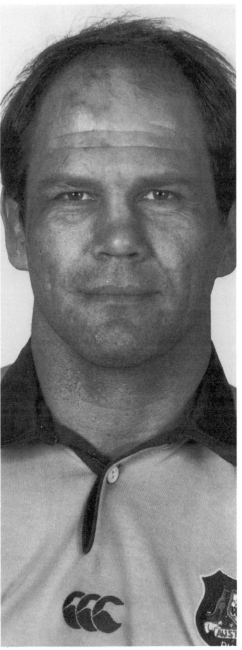

Peter FitzSimons – "moved" by the occasion.

players are about were people out there to believe we are in it for ourselves, for what is in it for us in some nebulous material way. Peter FitzSimons, the scholarly Wallaby lock whose very appearance is proof of the proposition that you really can educate gorillas, tells a beautiful story which places the emotion of the game alongside the bruising physical reality of it. Writing in the *Daily Telegraph* Peter says he had been waxing lyrical to his old mate Tommy Lawton, the vast Wallaby hooker, about how "moving" he had found it donning the Australian jersey (presumably for the first time) and singing the national anthem before playing a provincial game in Canada. He expected Tommy to slap him on the shoulder and say something like, "Yes, mate, that was really 'moving' for me, too."

Instead, Lawton snorted and said, "Mate, I'll tell you what moving is. Moving will be when you play a test match in France and the 15 of you can only just hear the tune of the anthem against the voices of the 70,000 Froggies that are screaming for your blood. You all belt it out anyway and you line up to receive the kick-off and you see this little sliver of white coming straight at you, end over end, like it's in slow motion, and you take it and get belted by four of them, but your mates close ranks to protect you and you drive them backwards and you form the first scrum with your blood just trickling down your nose on to your lip and your eyebrow swelling up and you can see the grass about three inches from your eyeball and you feel this massive heave coming from behind you, and that, that's what 'moving' is, mate."

And, says Peter, it happened just like Lawton said right down to the trickling blood and the swollen eyebrow.

However, the actuality apart, Peter's confession that he was "moved" by his first international experience with the anthem, the jersey and so on, stands up well to less cynical scrutiny in the experience of most test players. To some, and they include myself, the emotion of the occasion does persist even though you're busting your bladder to get on with the game and the cuts, bruises and dislocations that go with it. The players are not the automatons who scrum, kick, jump or score tries by pressing an internal button that activates them to do those jobs. They are guys with their country at heart.

However fashionable it may become from time to time to knock the game from its pedestal rugby is part of a New Zealand sporting ingredient which more than anything else encourages a sense of nationhood. It comes through Todd and Charisma, Hillary, Snell and Walker, Crowe and Sutcliffe, Lovelock, McDonald and Fergusson, McLaren and Hulme, Whineray and Kirwan...they are all flows from the reservoir to which New Zealanders in their geographical isolation turn for sustenance.

7

Pressures and hazards

If there has been one question more persistently prodded into my chest by blunt forefingers than any other since the World Cup it is: "OK then, Foxy. So why the hell did we go on spinning the ball so the bloody Aussies could keep on knocking us over?" It's a fair question. It happened because the message came out from the bench late in the first spell: "Attack out wide." So we did and we went on and on attacking out wide. I would not say the intent of the message was wrong. We were, after all, 13 points down and had we scored quickly through those tactics we could then have pulled back to a more conservative plan, certainly one which would have been more demanding on the Wallabies' resources. Were we to play the game again I'm sure we would have the ball in the air behind them, placing pressure on a variety of kicks. And we'd need to get into the game early so we wouldn't be battering away with the sort of 50-50 catch-up passes which place a team at such risk. We would not be in there, either, with our capacity to support guys like JK slashed back by players, like myself, carrying injury. I have pondered long and hard the events of the World Cup and the preparations for it. Hindsight, a marvellously convenient vehicle, tells me we persisted to a fault in endeavouring to play the sort of game we made so effective in 1987-88-89 while not being equipped with the players to sustain it. Everyone – players, coaches, public, media – were so excited by that expansive formula based on speed in the backs and mobility in the forwards. We tried to carry it on because there was pressure to do it.

With the introduction of new players we should have taken time out to sit down and work through the areas of change. Different strengths now, different skills, a loss of the experience crucial at the very top level. What fresh patterns should we formulate based on our new limitations and our new strengths? What should be the new winning pattern? Marginal tuning to cover changed circumstances and new players. After all, that was what was done intensively leading up to the World Cup of 1987.

We had lost experience. In the rush of rugby I doubt that any of us realised the extent to which that was affecting our game. Maybe we should have said, "To hell with the critics. We have to pull in our horns. We are not now equipped to play the rugby everyone wants us to go on playing. Consequently, we are making unforced mistakes (which we were) and the quality of our performance is being judged on our mistakes while the positive things (which there were) are ignored."

We talk of pressures these days as if there were never pressures on the players of ages past. Their pressures were those which existed mainly inside the match and those were not much different than they are now. The pressures you may think we talk of ad nauseum these days are those which are extraneous to the playing of the game yet which have significant influence on the playing of the game. They are the pressures created through the passage of time, by the movement of the game into a strongly commercial environment and the demands the players are now under to make the commercial administration of the game viable. Those demands are becoming heavier and with that weight on the players there comes weight on their families and their employers. That weight means worry. It can, and has, meant the fracturing of marriages.

Oddly, the avalanche of test rugby in the last decade or so has been a party-pooper for the public. Test rugby used to be something of a rarity and because of that there was a sort of eighth-wonder aura about it for New Zealanders. Now tests are taken for granted. They have lost their eliteness and with that loss much of the wonder has gone. But the circle is vicious.

No tests, no revenue; no revenue, no rugby. There is scope, then, for a more aggressive, more imaginative drive for major sponsorship both at provincial and national level.

The simple, most constant pressure on New Zealand players is from a public insatiable not only for wins but in its demand for perfection. In 1990 our young players were thrust into a heavy international programme after only one tour's experience, to Wales and Ireland. Usually it takes much longer for composure to come.

I guess in a curious way we created the rod for our own backs. We had been through that halcyon period of 50 games unbeaten, 23 tests unbeaten, a level of success not achieved before. We were getting bouquets, but what the media and the public saw as near-perfection was never near enough for us. We were never happy enough with what in most respects were seen to be performances of quality and style. Among ourselves we said such things as, "It's not the quantity it's the quality" and then went out chasing perfection. We were happier winning by one point playing as we wanted than by 20 playing below that standard. And, having established that benchmark, so we set the stage for disillusionment when, in trying to do the same things with new players, the mistakes came. Maybe as a team we were not as confidently patient as we had been, always with an eye to the last 20 minutes when we would make our charge. We were not establishing our ground rules through the graft of the forwards and the target moves to set ourselves up for the final quarter.

I do not blame the new players for we were all guilty of error. Consciously or not, established players were feeling the pinch maybe even more than the new and there was evidence that tiredness of mind – and, probably, of body – had infiltrated our system.

Pressures? There were others. It was pressure on coaches and players when the call came for some indefinable new ingredient in our rugby because rugby league was hammering at us. All the talk was of rugby league on television, the impact it was making and what rugby union had to do to combat it as a spectacle. Comparisons were made between the action in selected Winfield Cup highlights and rugby union games. There were committees to consider rule changes and suddenly rugby union was running scared of something it did not need to fear other than as a magnificent marketing spectacle, far beyond the ken of rugby union marketing. It is clear, however, that as the New Zealand rugby union pool of top players increasingly becomes a target for Australian rugby league clubs the black comedy of bringing our players through the development system and preparing them, in effect, for big careers as league players will have to be addressed.

I know the implicit call for more attractive rugby to fend off league at a critical time in our preparation for the World Cup was felt as an added obligation by Grizz and the players when they needed it like a hole in the head.

Always looming was "the All Black defence of the World Cup". The World Cup was in everyone's eyes but woe betide if we lost matches on the way to defending it. We were billed everywhere as world champions four years after we had won the title. The circumstances of players from 1987 had changed. Now we had a lot of married men with a lot of kids. Where rugby had been all-consuming now we were at a stage where we were thinking of life after rugby, career paths. We were putting our futures ahead of rugby where previously we had put rugby ahead of everything. It was happening because in a deteriorating economy we were worried. But we were being asked to play more and more rugby and expectations of us were getting higher and higher. Achieving a fair balance between rugby, family and work became virtually impossible.

The England captain, Will Carling, claimed New Zealand players lived off rugby, that we spent all day and every day either training for it or playing it. The total professionals. That is, of course, either the most ignorant or the most mischievous load of hogwash. Perhaps it was designed to draw attention away from the financial acrobatics by which English clubs and players can claim on the one hand to be the purest of the pure while on the other doing professional book-balancing acts which would leave a crooked accountant green with envy.

Will Carling – the ultimate judge of professionalism.

Kieran (The Colt) Crowley – a committed servant of the game.

For most of us it's after-hours rugby. We do participate in commercial activities but we are not rewarded for playing rugby. We would be one of the least professional teams in the world, most certainly behind Australia, France, England and Italy and probably on a par with Ireland and Wales.

I have pointed to the significant brake placed on our midfield strike-power by the loss of Gallagher, Ridge, Schuster and Stanley, the limitations we were then placed under in calling our moves. Craig Innes for Stanley was, of course, predictable. Craig had Joe's power while still, naturally, having to develop his commanding use of the ball and his anticipation of opportunities. Walter Little came in for Schuster, again a most gifted player needing time to become as stable as Schuster in a demanding position. He, in turn, gave way to Bernie McCahill for the reason of Bernie's distribution skill and stability. It is of point that Walter and Craig did not have the long-term advantage of being able to work in collaboration with a fullback like Gallagher. To that extent they were thrown in the deep end when options became limited. Kieran Crowley came in for Gallagher and as a technician he was among the very best. Crowley always gave everything to every game and he did have the ability to construct tries by high skill – witness that precise chip ahead and the regather at full gallop in the first test against Scotland at Carisbrook in 1990. A gem of a try. Kieran and I go away back. In 1978 Auckland Grammar played Sacred Heart with Kieran at fullback. He beat us single-handedly. We were all over Sacred Heart like a rash but we couldn't score points. They came into our half three times and Kieran kicked three good goals. It was my only loss in 60-odd games for Grammar and we reckoned we were out-numbered – 15 players and what other side could God be on but Sacred Heart? When Kieran first came back into the All Blacks after Gallagher had gone he played probably his finest rugby, staunch as ever and conscious of the All Black requirement to attack from fullback. But the search for a Gallagher-style re-placement was compulsive and Kieran did not have the legs for it. In most other aspects he was a more complete player than Kipper and it was not the absence of Kipper's pace alone which militated against the All Blacks playing the expansive game they were desperately seeking. The loss of other players was part of that equation.

So Terry Wright became our fullback and, while not being Gallagher through the middle, he was, with his pace running on the outside, a threat to any opposition.

Terry's speed was the All Black factor the Aussies say they feared. When he was injured severely enough to keep him out of the semi-final that fear element, that need to manufacture the means to contain him, thereby thinning up their defences else-where, evaporated and we were left in a jam. We prepared for the game with the idea of settling early then opening wide with Terry's speed outside JK. It was a critical factor in our game plan. So, who to replace him? Shayne Philpott, the utility, was also injured. John Timu had filled in quite outstandingly, I felt, against Canada and he must have been considered, with Va'aiga Tuigamala coming in on the wing. So it was Timu or a specialist replacement.

The decision was for a replacement and the choice came down to two players: Crowley, who had expressed his disillusionment with rugby when he was not selected in the original World Cup party, and Greg Cooper, who had played so assertively for Otago that winter and who had the feeling and the means for the midfield burst. I understand that had Cooper been in Italy, where it was assumed he would be, he would have been brought in to the squad. As it eventuated, he was not and the man they finally went for back home was Crowley, the dependable Colt.

So Crowley, without rugby for three weeks, had to come in to a match which, whatever the result, would be a pressure-match for everyone, a match played with pace and power. It was a huge requirement on a player without recent rugby and one who had not been involved with the team for the rest of the World Cup campaign.

It had been a campaign of highs, middles and lows. Through a seeding system and draw which owed something to northern hemisphere subjectivity and something to Mickey Mouse in about equal proportions we were "programmed" to meet Australia in a semi-final, thus ensuring Twickenham would not be sullied by an antipodean shoot-out in a final most people considered would have been a true expression of world rugby strengths. Writing in the *Daily Telegraph* as England cruised to another Five Nations championship this year, John Reason said:

"We should remember that though New Zealand are in an unaccustomed state of flux themselves, they wiped out England in the World Cup far more easily than Australia did. What is more, I have no doubt whatever that they would have done it again, and perhaps rather more easily, if they and not Australia had played England in the final at Twickenham. The World Cup draw was a fudge and England were the beneficiaries."

That excerpt had added point coming from Reason, a hard-nosed critic who has a reputation in New Zealand as a writer not moved to special elation, let alone sycophancy, over New Zealand rugby through the years. It is of note, too, because the reaction of the British media to our beating of England in the World Cup opener varied almost to the point of the ridiculous. The former Scotland and British Isles lock Gordon Brown, a comments man on television, thought our performance against England magnificent. Perhaps he may have over-stated the case but from our view of it, as players, we did to England what we had to do.

Another *Daily Telegraph* writer, columnist Michael Calvin, was much less impressed. Rugby had to come to terms, he said, with the fact that New Zealand, its best team, was also its worst advertisement... "they instinctively strangle important matches by playing result rugby." It was an intriguing observation following a match like that against England in which the home team, with a wealth of lineout possession in the first spell, did their level best to choke themselves with it. Certainly, we helped them along the path of that particular strangulation but the genesis of it was in their own minds, their own approach which, on the strangling scale, was suicidal. Had they taken a gallows on to the middle of Twickenham, hitched the rope to a skyhook, tied the noose around their necks and jumped they could not more graphically have illustrated their state of mind. What we did was save them the effort of jumping by giving them a shove.

As to playing "result rugby" I would have thought that desirable end should have been in England's mind, too, for the opening engagement of rugby's ultimate expo.

Against England we played what most simply could be called traditional All Black rugby to win. I think we played it well against a considerable backdrop of conjecture – not to say suggestion – that we should "throw" that match and thus avoid the troublesome business of having to get past Australia in a semifinal. As one writer over there put it: "Don't put it past these Kiwis to take a dive. Getting back to Twickenham for the final would see all of New Zealand forgive them the loss." So much that is unrefined bullshit does emerge when journalists sit down and try to turn an obtuse angle into an acute observation. Those who espoused that cause had to be among the real oddballs of rugby. Certainly they had no understanding of the temper of rugby players, and I make that point on behalf of all rugby players, not just the All Blacks.

Consider Michael Jones, self-drafted out of Sunday rugby because of his commitment to God, being confronted with a proposal that he should contribute to a deliberate loss on one of the rare Saturdays he would get to play the game! Michael's inclusion in the team was the subject of some withering criticism, but never more withering than when we lost to Australia. It was unreservedly justifiable to take Michael. You have only to study his contribution to the game against England to understand why. When we called the move which resulted in Michael scoring the game's only try, it was he who engineered a scrum-switch with Alan Whetton and from that point on the try was his. It was a move we had polished up after first using it in the second test against Argentina earlier in the year but the Jones factor at Twickenham was purely Jones-inspired. In Argentina it had Graeme Bachop on the loop, finding space before sending JK away. At Twickenham, Graeme looped Innes and threw a long pass to JK and when he was covered by Jonathon Webb there, on order, was Jones running irresistibly inside him.

Michael Jones is one of that rare breed, a footballing freak. There are two freaks in world rugby, one Michael the other Laurie Daley, the Canberra Raiders and Australian league fiveeighths, both stunningly skilled with speed, vision, anticipation. Jones is such a virtuoso he could play in the midfield at inter-

Michael Jones – the greatest of all?

national level. With a bit of a familiarity course, he would make a great centre. And he would also make a great rugby league player just as Daley would make a superb union player. Daley has such balance, such a sharp perception of the half-chance.

The rare in-built quality they both have is an instinct for the game. I have listened to old-timers talk of Bert Cooke, the slip of a man who was an All Black five-eighths of the roaring '20s. Undoubtedly a freak and again, instinct, balance, vision, speed, anticipation - and the greatest of these is instinct. Cooke became as brilliant in league as he was in union for nothing is beyond such wondrous players.

It would have been grossly unfair had Michael not been selected for the World Cup on the basis that his religious conviction denied him playing on Sundays. Yes, it would have been a huge plus to have had him in the semi-final but were I a selector faced with the same decision again tomorrow I would take him. He is rugby's fourth dimension, the All Blacks' fourth dimension and, as such, his place in the team was indisputable. When there was some suggestion that the All Blacks' August test against South Africa might be played on a Sunday I thought immediately of Michael and what an all-round tragedy it would be first for the All Blacks to be without him for this momentous match and second for the South African rugby public to be denied a test match view of the player who is arguably the best in any position in world rugby. His performance while he was on in the match we played at Onewa Domain, North Harbour's head-quarters, before leaving for the World Cup last year was one of the greatest 40 minutes of rugby by an individual I have ever seen. Nothing was beyond him.

I questioned the advisability of that game on the grounds of its potential for injury so close to the cup tournament and, reflecting on it, perhaps it gave us a false impression of what was to come and how we could deal with it. There we had two teams trying to play the same sort of broad-vision rugby, not a planned strategy for one team to play the sort of rugby we would anticipate the Aussies might play in the World Cup. But I guess those are straws in the wind.

Would Michael Jones have made a difference at Lansdowne Road? In the view of one New Zealand fan he would. Writing from home the Jones-follower said, "If you think about it, Michael, it will actually be Monday morning over here. So go ahead and play."

Twickenham for the opening match was buzzing. In many ways, not least in the manner of the draw, this had become the key to a place in the final. The losing team would have to negotiate France and Scotland on the way back to Twickenham,

The challenge to England – Twickenham, World Cup, 1991.

the winner with, most significantly, Australia. Had we lost to England I suggest we would have played the final against Australia. Pie in the sky? True. But there would not have been an All Black who did not believe in our ability to deal with France and Scotland.

England had a fine tight-five with the best ball-winning ability by far of the five nations. There was, however, a lack of mobility in the loose forwards, no one to provide a Jones-like link between forwards and backs. Most of the backline were talented players but playing to such a taut, restrictive recipe that there was little, we felt, to fear from them. So it proved. Yet it was the style, I am sure, which offered them their best chance of beating Australia.

It was under the severest criticism of their dour tactics from their own media that England was pressured into change for the final. It was an ill-fated aberration. The team – quaintly, considering the distaste of the British media for losing teams – was lauded for losing to Australia with style, for finally giving such fine players as Jeremy Guscott, Carling and Rory Underwood their heads. The fact was that the media, having pressed for the change, then had nowhere to go when it did not work. The problem was that at no stage of the cup tournament had England prepared themselves to play this sort of rugby and the country which least of all they should have chosen to play it against was Australia. Consequently, their passing and handling was erratic. There was an at-all-costs lack of control. Exciting it was but England's best chance of beating Australia was by clinging doggedly to the game-plan which took them to the final.

Throughout the tournament England's attitudes and posturings made them unpopular with other teams. There was a lack of winning grace. The Italians were incensed at England's non-stop sledging about their offside play. Yet the Italians related strongly to us after our match, not because their propensity to play offside had changed but because we didn't belabour them with it and praised them for getting within 10 points of us. When England beat France they complained piercingly about France's tactics which, they said, led to the game's bitterness. This rather over-looked that the foulest of the fouls in the match was the kick delivered by one of England's loose forwards. Even after the final they bitched about David Campese reaching through to knock the ball down as England attacked out to his wing with Rory Underwood to receive the final pass. They cried foul long and tiresomely and the associated claim it should have been a penalty try was fairytale stuff.

In the meantime, our own campaign ducked and dived...against the United States we tried just about everything going when we should have been settling the game down early, committing the opposition in close before cutting loose. The rash of mistakes, many of them unforced, became infective and although the final score was 46-6 with eight tries the performance overall was such that no one could take pride from it as a team performance. On the other hand, the Americans, inspired by their skipper, Kevin Swords, harried and harassed us, tackled themselves to a stand-still and left the field victors in their way.

The Italians tested us in just about every way in the book. They bombed us, they tackled us, they ran at us. There were Italians under every blade of grass on Leicester's Welford Road ground. Good on them. Their performance was archetypal under-dog – a classic of the genre. It was Rocky Balboa, the Italian Stallion, getting in there against the heavyweight champ and giving him hell – not winning, but giving him hell. Good on them, but frustrating for us. We were finding it impossible to take control at our great strength, the second phase. There was an almost studied refusal to let rucks develop beyond birth and what with the ball-killing compulsion of most northern hemi-sphere teams we were often left fuming that we were not able to set up the platform from which, classically, we are at our attacking best.

What the Italians and the Americans had shown was that,

Ball in hand against the Italian Stallions. Zinny Brooke in support.

given the incentive, there is a wealth of rugby on the up in so-called second-tier countries. Most dramatically in this World Cup the evidence of this was coming from the Western Samoans who were taking the tournament and its followers by storm. Just as the Fijians emerged as a rugby nation of real consequence in the 1987 World Cup so did the Samoans in 1991. The challenge for the Fijians was to sustain that progress. Regrettably, they haven't. The challenge now is the same for Western Samoa. It will be difficult for them. Like the Fijians they play the game aggressively with hard tackling and with elements of intimidation. But they are a gift to rugby for their natural skills, their strength, their love of the game and their warmth. Fiji has not had the luxury of having most of its players coming through the New Zealand system and it is hard to accept that Samoans should have the opportunity of trying out for the All Blacks and, failing that, turning to Western Samoa for representation. They are marvellous for New Zealand rugby but it is not surprising that their multiple-choice has come under scrutiny.

Before the All Blacks' quarter-final against Canada there was something of an all-round bollocking from the coaches. It was time for it. We had not been producing the rugby with which we could approach a semi-final against Australia with any sort of confidence. Our error-rate was beyond acceptance and the lead

Rob Andrew searches for the posts – the World Cup opener at Twickenham.

had to come from the senior players. It was time for a few thousand well-aimed words. In these circumstances John Hart has a distinctive, sharp-edged intensity and a vocabulary-flow befitting a company executive if not a meeting of the board. Grizz Wyllie is a blunt street-fighter, every pungent word a kick in the groin, every scowl an elbow in the teeth and every curse a Liverpool kiss. Between the two of them they made the earth lurch and it was with ringing eardrums that we went out in harrowing conditions in Lille, of all places, to justify ourselves against Canada.

It was a good game for us and a good came for Canada. We just about got it right. Given a dry day we could have taken the game apart. We restored some old-fashioned values, gave ourselves platforms to launch set-piece moves and scored five tries. But the Canadians gave us heaps, exactly the sort of tough, physical workout we needed. And they scored two good tries to bow out of the World Cup in style and to proclaim they will be harder yet in 1995.

While we were having the gutsy, satisfying game with Canada, across the sea in Ireland the Aussies went to the edge of the abyss, teetered and, as every man, woman and child in the delirious Dublin crowd gave them a shove, they swivelled like a 15-man Campo, stepped back into the game and scored. We were as near as dammit going to Dublin to play Ireland. What a day that would have been have been have been...

"I'll shoot it." Referee Ken McCartney of Scotland gives me a familiar sign, v Australia, Eden Park, 1991.

Wasting bubbles. Richard Loe shows no respect for France's fine product after we have beaten Australia at Eden Park, 1991.

The eternal autograph hunt at the New Zealand trial, Rotorua, 1991.

Summing up the options against England, Twickenham, 1991. Maybe to run?
Never.

Something to chase. The bomb on the way and Zinzan Brooke, Richard Loe,
Gary Whetton and Steve McDowell frothing for the hunt.

Nantes revisited,1990, and here come some of our points.

Graeme Bachop has given me the opportunity to feed the line, second test v Australia, 1990.

Puzzle: pick the bewildered Frenchman, La Rochelle, with physio David Abercrombie, 1990.

Loneliness is kicking practice at Twickenham. The scene in the week before the World Cup opener, 1991.

The grubber-kick for Sean Fitzpatrick, the renowned winger, who will get on to it and score the try against France, Lancaster Park, 1989.

Being hit by a French train. Laurent Rodriguez let's me have it, Eden Park, second test, 1989.

8

Dare not lose

There's a television commercial for Minties. The number on
the back of the rugby player is unmistakeable. It says 10. A
pregnant figure. One moment you see it as the player runs
in to kick the ball. The next moment you see no number because
the player is arse-up in the middle of a bundle of television
equipment and television people. It is embarrassing for the
player because he has just explained scientifically to the television producer that, as the sequence is to be shot on concrete, he
is wearing rubber studs. You understand, he has just said, that
were I to have worn metal studs on concrete I would finish arse-
up to everyone's acute displeasure, not to mention my own
embarrassment and pain. Then, having established his profound
knowledge of which ever of the sciences covers metal studs on
concrete, the player runs in to kick and goes arse-up anyway.
When they have all recovered, they tell the player it is very funny
but not quite what they had in mind.

The event is the shooting of Auckland's A-Team commercial
for the 1991 season. The film-cut which disproves the theory of
the infallibility of rubber studs on concrete is recovered and the
"It's Moments Like These" boys bring it to me and ask if they may
use it in their next television commercial. I agree. Have I done the
right thing? Assuredly I have brought pleasure into the lives of
those who prefer to see me arse-up. But my wife and children
laugh at it, too...and my friends. Fitzpatrick says he judges it to
be very flattering, by far the most becoming picture of me he has
ever seen.

It's Moments Like These...for all their recuperative powers, I
doubt that a packet of Minties would have done the job at
Lansdowne Road. After the match I felt about as uplifted as the

day Richard Loe sat on me, protectively, at the bottom of a ruck during a Ranfurly Shield match at Eden Park. As his Waikato mates contested the ball and me in about equal shares I saw, then felt, this vast bum descend and then engulf me. Not an Auckland bum, but Loe's Waikato bum. Not, I might say, your classical Elle bum. More your rhino-tending-to-elephant bum. Then, though the sensitivities were severely shaken, I heard his voice rumbling down and, it seemed to me, emerging from a surprising orifice for a voice. Loe said, "Don't get here again, Foxy. I'm a thoughtful man but once is enough." What, in his concern for my welfare, he did not consider was whether I would much have preferred a scrape or two of Waikato studs to obliteration by bum.

I have talked of the state of depression in the New Zealand dressing-room immediately after the World Cup semi-final. It wasn't just the depression of loss, the end of a dream, exhaustion. There was already the ache of self-recrimination. The dreaded what-ifs and if-onlys. What if I had come off when I was injured? Maybe it would have brought some different dimension to the game. If only I could have got there to support JK that time. Not the stuff for the Mintie treatment so we clambered out of it on the back of a carton or two of the cold stuff.

The Aussies were humble and generous in victory and they judged us to be magnanimous and dignified in defeat. Grizz had gone to their dressing room immediately and moved among the players congratulating them individually on their performance. Not your gruff, disgruntled Grizz but a warm and sincere man. It was a gesture which stuck. When Grizz's book, *Grizz The Legend*, was to be launched Michael Lynagh was asked to be a part of the occasion. He couldn't come but, expressing his regret, he said normally he would walk blindfolded over broken glass to do anything for Grizz.

Recriminations were, of course, not all self-inflicted. There were those which were to be expected. There was one from an old All Black who could not believe that in that long lateral run across our defensive remnants, Campese was not touched by an All Black until he was about to plant the ball down. He might identify where it could have been done and by whom. We had not regrouped sufficiently after the first Australian thrust from the Farr-Jones Willie-away and the Lynagh set-up of second phase allowing Campese to take up the run against the flow of play. It was a masterpiece of planning. I would love to have been part of a similarly constructed try. That it should be seen as succeeding because of our reluctant defence denigrates the brilliance of it. Had we scored the try it would, presumably, have been magnificent and old All Blacks would not have been sniping at the Australian defence.

Campo on the way to his semi-final try; recrimination against the All Black defence.

We had changed our defensive pattern against the Australians at Eden Park in 1991. We went from a one-out defence – the first five-eighths on to the second, the second five-eighths to the centre, the centre to the wing – to a man-on-man. Generally from lineouts that means I ghost in behind, with the loosie looking after the opposing first five-eighths. When Lynagh appeared in the Dublin movement there was confusion for our midfield. He came from an angle, hidden from me, took the ball up and laid it back beautifully. What eventuated with Campo was classical wrong-footing of a defence still moving in the direction of the breakdown.

Perhaps we should have changed our attacking pattern. Maybe Bernie McCahill out to centre and Craig Innes in to second five-eighths? The big guy to push it at the Australian defence, to cause greater concern in closer? Maybe even to bring a bit of consternation to what was a finely-tuned, imperturbable defence system? Bernie to handle the distribution out wide? I have always felt that at second-phase time there is a case for the physically commanding player to be in closer. In the circumstances of the semi-final it would have been an option. No more than that; certainly not a sure-fire winning option. It was something we could have tried but didn't.

The Australian planning for the World Cup was text-book

Craig Innes in Tim Horan's grip – should he have been at second-five?

material and should be studied and digested by all other countries as they look toward 1995. Here is a country where, historically,
rugby union is constantly on the backfoot to league but has hung
in there tenaciously and emerged with players of the combative
turn of mind which reflects the struggle the game has had to hold
its ground. An Australian once wrote with resignation that
Australian rugby was of the nature that it would be beaten with
regularity by New Zealand but just from time to time in a good

year it would produce the team to beat New Zealand in a bad year. What has happened in the last couple of years could well be the undoing of that philosophy.

The trans-Tasman sporting rivalry is something which people scrutinising it from a world away, or even a continent away, could not hope to understand. It knows little of the acrimony – the detestation, if you like – which flows between the French and the English. By nature, I would judge Australians to be more nationalistically aggro than New Zealanders but no more competitive. Australians would respond to that, I am sure, by calling in overwhelming evidence that New Zealanders are further up themselves than Australians but with less cause. The fact is that it would not matter whether you had a red-back spider racing a weta up a dunny wall, the sense of rivalry would be white-hot.

As rugby players we have deep respect for them. In 1989 they came to New Zealand with a couple of youngsters named Phil Kearns and Tony Daly in the front row. At centre they had a 19-year-old in his first season of senior football, Tim Horan. They introduced another kid named Jason Little to the midfield on the tour of France the same year. The grand plan was under way and faith in the young players was unwavering. They shrugged off defeat as a learning process, they went after fitness in the same way the All Blacks had done, they settled on a game that suited them and new selections were always with an eye to the contest the World Cup would become.

The Aussies have always had backs of talent and sometimes of great brilliance. They have not always hitched that talent to disciplined team patterns. They have lacked the grafting forwards upon which to found their attack. Alan Jones changed their rugby by going for the big men to mend the problems in set pieces. But they initiated another problem. They were big men lacking mobility and the mind for 80 minutes of hard yakka. Bob Dwyer was prepared to sacrifice a little of the size to get the men who could move and the men with the will. He found the right balance with players like Rod McCall, John Eales and Peter FitzSimons. That in Eales he would introduce to the team in the year of the World Cup a 21-year-old lock who would become as much a key to Australian performance as Farr-Jones or Lynagh or Horan is typical of his perception and boldness. And that he would accept from New Zealand, without embarrassment, Willie Ofahengaue, a gift of petty bureaucratic intransigence, and turn him into a potent World Cup force, was really rubbing it in. When they lost such a key player as Tim Gavin through injury I thought they would be made to struggle. But Willie O found a gear and a temperament I doubted he had and Simon Poidevin shed age like a cloak. Simon epitomises what New Zealand-Australia

Simon Poidevin – shed age like a cloak.

rugby is all about. He has retired at least twice but cannot resist the lure of another body-trial at the bottom of a New Zealand ruck.

The Australian backs, as a unit, are not as creative as they once were. They do not need to be. They have the world's best half-back and they are quite superb individually in the sliding defence system. Where our defence is based on getting up and knocking men over, theirs drifts across, Lynagh on to my pass at the second five-eighths, Horan to the centre, Little to the extra man position outside centre. So you have a team with a strong tight five, winning its share of ball, getting into the right attacking area behind a top kicker, applying pressure and getting points. You put a champion goal-kicker on that base and you have a hell of a rugby team. By 1991 the Aussies could absorb pressure where previously we could almost always crack them in the last 15 minutes. They learned from New Zealand that only 80-minute fitness is good enough, that the first thing to suffer when players became tired is the ability to think. They became much more adept at scoring points when they placed themselves in try-scoring situations and when the opposition got into the same situation they were able to deny them with that pig-headed defence.

The Aussies sat on leads. They never really blitzed sides in the big games. They went for their points early, tried to command possession, turned around with their lead, placed the utmost faith in their defensive line and resolved not to concede penalties. They would concede a ruck rather than concede a penalty in it and the same applied to the lineouts.

Our loss to Australia at Lansdowne Road was comprehensive. I say this because there has been a tendency to point to the New Zealand backs as having lost the match. It was in the backs' inability to break the Aussie line that the loss was most graphically underlined but it was a team loss and you would not find an All

Black forward who would shrink from a share of the responsibility. Having said that, I repeat the tight five are everything to a team. They receive few of the accolades. They are buried, heads down, bums up, the numbers on their backs not seen. Everything is linked to what the tight five have done. They are the hidden force of rugby. When we are able to play that broad, expressive game everyone loves, the sweaty tight five watch grimly as the Chanel sharpshooters out in the threequarters receive the bouquets with modest smiles. When the game is stilted and erratic and the backs can do little right the tight five smile without remorse because they know the scales are about to be balanced. The backs will get hell but the tight five, again, will be ignored.

Willie O – Australian by bureaucratic decree.

Statistics (and I apologise for reverting to them) show that in the quarter-final, semi-finals, play-offs for third and fourth, and final New Zealand's possession was clearly beyond that of Australia, England and Scotland and notably in second phase where Australia won 28 pieces, England 58, New Zealand 101 and Scotland 61. The fly-half distribution figures show that Australia kicked 45 times and passed 39, England 47 and 48, New Zealand 30 and 82 and Scotland 31 and 37. So, they seem to say, we did make a welter of the passing game...we had, indeed, become predictable.

The English media received our loss with, again, quaint variations of values. Where some gloated that the All Black era was over and thank God for that, others pointed to the end of a great era with appreciation of what the All Blacks had achieved and given to other countries and to rugby football. The *Daily Mail*, through Jeff Powell, could find nothing good to say while judging that England would not concede to Australia "as readily as New Zealand laid down their legend." He wallowed in this anticipation: "The free spirits of Australia will meet the Grand Slammers of England in a contrast of styles, a spectacle rendered

Frank Keating – gave us a fair crack of the whip.

all the brighter now that the All Black shadow has been lifted from the headquarters of the 15-man game."

Twickers, he might have added, had been starved of the 15-man game for years by its own spiritual progeny.

Frank Keating, the much-decorated writer of *The Guardian*, was less priggish by far and infinitely more enlightening in a review which, while handsomely giving the Australians their due, gave New Zealand a fair crack of the whip as well... "The wings at Lansdowne Road, all four of them, had the ball in their hands more often than a slip fielder at catching practice. All 14 runners on either side were bristling with eagerness, expectant for the ball, demanding it."

In *The Mail on Sunday* Patrick Collins wrote: "New Zealand departed this World Cup with only the medals they give for third place. Yet that ranking says little about their real influence...the truth is that the small country at the foot of the world has set the standards for rugby through generations. Not merely by murderous forward attrition, nor by romantic back play but by the intelligent co-ordination of those qualities. The names of the great ones have already passed into legend, and now the owners of those names must follow. But if we really have seen the last of the Brothers Whetton, of Kirwan and Fox, of the front row trinity, McDowell, Loe and Fitzpatrick, then we should not let them go without a respectful word of thanks..."

Collins reminds his readers that New Zealand's time will come again – "in about four years, I'd say."

The players did not expect accolades from media which had long since branded us as arrogant, unapproachable, humourless and uncooperative (which adds up to a fearsome burden for 26 pretty normal jokers to carry around among people who are inclined to believe at least part of what they read).

It did seem to us from the beginning that the price of being tagged world champions was that sections of the English media would set out to cut us down, treat accuracy as a discardable inconvenience if inaccuracy gave them a more sensational quote or headline. We were made conscious very quickly that for some unfathomable reason our record of success made us vulnerable to the peripheral snipers of the press. Certainly this knowledge did nothing for our relationships with the English media. You might say we became overly sensitive. We would say we became bloody suspicious. If, within that scenario, there emerged an impression of arrogance I would accept that.

That having been said, I would add that I wish we had been able to handle our media relations with the organised aplomb of the Australians. Their contact with journalists was deftly conducted by an experienced newspaperman, Greg Campbell, officially attached to the party. Goodwill flowed. I understand the All Black management was offered the same sort of facility by the New Zealand Rugby Union but declined it. If it is so, it was a fateful misjudgement. The demands of the media in an event like the World Cup were predictably intense, predictably outside the understanding of ordinary management. What should have been a full-time concern was treated by New Zealand as a bit of a nuisance to be overcome by undefined, haphazard means. The result was, of course, a public relations disaster. It would be a blind man who could not now accept that.

As the media become more and more demanding we have to instigate repair work so we may better understand what they require. Before television, the traditional media, radio and newspapers, were largely content to inform, to describe the matches, opinion being secondary to applied knowledge in giving accurate descriptions of the games. With television the public were able to see the events of a match unfold and it became a requirement on the newspapers to go for the angles, to go after family stories, to probe into the personal lives of the players.

Opinion writing is all very well provided fact is at the foundation of it. It is self-indulgent, lazy journalism to float opinion which often has its roots in rumour or in ignorance. It may be significant that what in this country is seen to be a serious deterioration in player-media relationships coincided with the advent of tabloid-style angled journalism which found a receptive audience. That may be one arc of a vicious circle in that badly-angled journalism is the result of the comparative isolation of the players.

The New Zealand Rugby Union would do well to organise a seminar to be attended by players' representatives, by managers, coaches and the media to discuss both sides of the equation. I have made myself available to the media at the drop of a hat –

Alan Whetton – judged and executed on television.

perhaps even to a fault – but generally among the players there is no feeling for what the media are about. What we do not need is the sort of well-meant but half-baked media meeting organised by the New Zealand union in March of 1991 which was so facile it served more to confuse than clarify. It skated over the real issues like media accessibility to the players. Instead of the constant squabbling over dressing-room access after games, the microphones under noses when we come off the field knackered, there has to be a smoother way based on mutual understanding. Somewhere along the line, and the sooner the better, there has to be an exchange of information. Rugby is so big in this country, so much the game of the people, that it would be irresponsible – not to say self-destructive – were the administration not to take a lead in setting these things right.

The players felt strongly about the trial by television of Alan Whetton following the incident which resulted in Stephen Bachop's head injuries. It seemed television guru Paul Holmes set himself up as a hanging judge in a manner which seemed more anti-rugby than anti-Whetton. He became prosecutor, judge and jury in circumstances which, had they involved criminal activity, would have been in contempt. He was not alone in shrugging off the protestation of "the accused" that what had happened was by accident. The sufferers in such cases of persecution are not just the players. Far beyond the feeling of the players the families suffer. I know that AJ's mother was deeply affected by what became a campaign.

When the case did, in fact, go to trial before a committee of the New Zealand Rugby Union including two lawyers, John Dowling and Tim Gresson QC, the act was found to be unintentional. But having decided that, the committee then barred him for three weeks. I am only a layman but that seemed to me to be an odd way to dispense justice.

I am glad to say the wounds inflicted by the approach of Paul Holmes have healed. The Whettons themselves buried the hatchet not in Holmes's skull, which might have been their inclination a year before, but by inviting him to their book launch. Holmes responded warmly and goodwill reigned. I do believe he may have a closer understanding now of rugby – certainly an affinity with the players of the game. As part of the World Cup lead-up he needed a Holmes goal-kicking segment and I was there to teach him the gentle art. I would say that on the McDowell-Loe scale (max. 10) he would score a well-merited 3. McDowell and Loe unashamedly set the benchmark by their own goal-kicking expertise at 3.5. Finally, I organised Paul to kick around the corner but with the toe, a revolutionary concept which is unlikely to take hold other than among smallish, bespectacled television personalities whose co-ordination and rhythm are more of the tongue than of the body. The magic of editing converted Paul into a goal-kicker of about 4.5, a monumental tribute to electronic wizardry.

I had wondered what it would be like when we came home from the World Cup. Having been made pretty sensitive in the past to the eagerness with which some New Zealanders leap on to the rumour bandwagons once someone or other sets them rolling I suspected there would be something similar, something personally directed at a few. Perhaps it was not, then, surprising that the two people sorted out for the treatment were Gary Whetton and myself. After all, were we not the "conspirators" who had dealt to Buck? Were we not, as captain and backline tactician, the arch-criminals behind the defeat of the All Blacks at Lansdowne? It was as arch-criminals we were dealt with by those who had to have scapegoats upon whom to vent their spleen at having suffered, along with the players, defeat.

I could accept as sincerely-felt, criticism which came from those who had the gumption to sign their names. I could accept, without question, that for whatever reason my performance in the World Cup semi-final was less than I had hoped for and worked for. But by far the greatest volume of sound and fury came from those who bombarded the talk-back waves, anonymous executioners talking from a vast background of ignorance. They have my contempt. Thank God I had the support of many who are not given to ringing radio stations or writing to newspapers for I believe they spoke for New Zealand's largely-silent majority.

When the time came for New Zealand trials in 1992 Gary Whetton was not considered to be one of the top 10 locks in the country, a make-believe assessment. Nor, till he initiated a discussion with one of the selectors, was he given an inkling that in the selectors' view he had served his time. He did not deserve

Gary Whetton – by right and dignity deserved a New Zealand trial.

the humiliation of peremptory dismissal after 11 years as an All Black. He did not deserve, as a player, to be discarded without a trial. It is the sort of treatment which has been meted out to some other outstanding All Blacks and captains of the past. I would have thought that by 1992 we would have escaped that dark age of boorishness.

9

Ghost-busting

To ensure this is a rounded story of my life it is important I should disclose details of my secret career as a bareknuckle fighter. Of prime importance, of course, was the biggest slug-fest of my career when, fighting as Fractious Foxy, I took on Bullocky Buck, the North Harbour Terror, in 1990. Blood? You should have seen the blood! Yes, and guts, too. Blood and guts all over the walls. That Buck! What a slugger. I hit him with some vicious uppercuts around the kneecaps but he came back like an enraged lion, baled me up in a corner, leaned all over me till I was totally stuffed, picked me up, hung me by the singlet to a coat-hook and hit me with everything including Stevie McDowell's jockstrap – which Stevie happened to be wearing at the time. If it hadn't been for Grizz Wyllie I was a gonner, the end of a glittering career. But Grizz grabbed Buck in the dreaded crutch-hold perfected by the Canterbury forwards of the '70s, dragged him off me, and with a delicate head-butt here and an exquisite knee in the bollocks there had Bullocky Buck in trouble. But, at the last gasp, Bullocky lifted himself to his awesome, aggro best and battered Grizz around the ears with a haka. And Grizz, not to be bested, snarled, "That's the last time you play for New Zealand, Shelford!" How does that grab you? This is the first indecent exposure of the truth behind Buck Shelford's demise as captain of the All Blacks. I swear it is as near the truth as the rumours which fled through the country when Buck was dropped after the second test against Scotland at Eden Park.

Just to recap...after the test Buck was asked about the tactics. He said Foxy was his eyes and ears in the backline. This meant, of course, that Buck was blaming Foxy for the poor performance. The enraged Foxy thereupon engaged Buck in a dressing-room fistfight. And Grizz, pissed-off with the whole show, had a knock-'em-down, drag-'em-out with Buck. Foxy then got among his Auckland mates and went to Grizz with this ultimatum: "If Buck's in the team count us out." Foxy, incidentally, had already conspired with Gary Whetton to sabotage Buck out of any decision-making in the Scotland test. So Grizz, upset to the point of tears by the ultimatum, dropped Buck and appointed Whetton captain.

It's a marvellous story but fiction from beginning to end. And as with all stories which are circulated with malice, people were hurt, reputations were dragged through the mire and something akin to hatred started to come through as the rumours went into galloping mode. Regrettably, not enough was done to stop them in their tracks and the more they went around and around the more people believed them – and embellished them.

First we should consider the background. Scotland: To my regret I have never played at Murrayfield. My only experience of playing Scotland is in New Zealand. But I have only admiration for the commitment they have to the game, for their ability, under Ian McGeechan, to plan incisively between matches, closing down their own weaknesses, preparing to exploit weaknesses they have pinpointed in the opposition – in this case the All Blacks. They can be as disruptive as any but are in for a fling when the occasion is there. What we have for the Scots and, we believe, they have for us is a respect which goes deeper than rugby. It comes through in our off-field relationship which, for us, is probably closer than with any other team.

McGeechan just might be the nicest chap in all of rugby but within the easy amiability there's a sharp, calculating rugby mind. They had in Gavin Hastings an awesome player at his best, so big, so positive. We played together in the Auckland University club the season following the 1987 World Cup and I contrived to give him only one shot at goal – and that because it was too far for me. They had a great loose forward unit in Finlay Calder, Derek White and John Jeffrey, a combative front row led by David Sole and Iain Milne and a fine lock in Chris Gray, gifted halves in Craig Chalmers and Gary Armstrong, a Kiwi with the great rugby name of Lineen in midfield...in fact, all-round the touring team of 1990 had strength.

When we beat Scotland 32-16 at Carisbrook on my 28th birthday we thought that was about as well as they could play but that we had plenty of improvement in us. Our error-rate was high. We were, of course, without Schuster and Gallagher and we had no Michael Jones. We were conscious there was much to be done and the dressing-room afterward was quite subdued for a winning team.

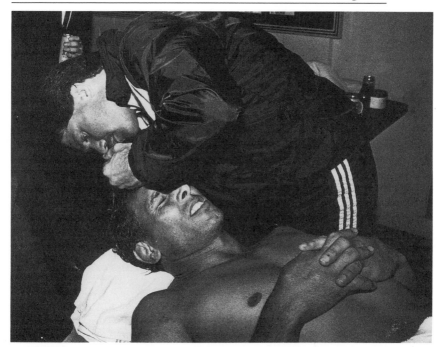

Buck Shelford being revived after my kinghit? No, just stitches without anaesthetic.

The weather at Eden Park for the second test was, as Queen Victoria used to say, inclement. Like bloody awful. Like strong, cold wind, sweeping showers, slippery on top. We had trained to exploit the weaknesses we had detected in the first test – as, for instance, opportunity on the blind side. While the ball was dry I reckoned we should be having a crack at our game plan. But McGeechan was ahead of the game. He had detected his team's vulnerability, too, and he had sealed-up the cracks and notably the one on the blind. There was a good old-fashioned get-stuffed approach from the Scots but they were well-organised with it. They built two top tries, one a planned jolt through our midfield and into clear air, obviously an area McGeechan had identified as one of defensive fluidity. They led us 18-9 at one stage and 18-12 at half-time. We restored wet-weather tactics and clawed back into the game to win it 21-18. In the dressing-room afterward there was quite a buzz. We had come from behind in a game which had threatened to get away from us so there were the ingredients of relief as well as the satisfaction of winning. In the media interview Buck was queried, critically, about our tactics. He said I was his eyes in the backline. This was snapped up as implied (at least) criticism of me. Knowing Buck, I doubt that was so. Grizz also questioned our tactics in the news conference. He came back to the dressing-room and told me it was not a criticism of me personally but reflective on the whole team. Later in his book he was to point to a lack of communication between the loose forwards and the backs. I think it is true, too, there were loose ends between Buck and Graeme Bachop.

On Sky television the following day I was asked about Buck's comment and the tactics of the day. I laughed and said, "Normally I'm criticised for kicking too much, now I'm criticised for running it." It was a throw-away line, no more than that. Buck's comments on a radio interview the same day fuelled the charge that he was being critical of me.

It was in that climate that the fist-fight rumours hit the airwaves. Buck and me. Buck and Grizz. I'm not into the business of fighting. Not even against guys my own size. I'm happy to be in the middle of a heavy-contact game but fighting is an awful waste of time and energy. And there is something slapstick, something ludicrously Marx Brothers, isn't there, about a Shelford-Fox set-to? Now Shelford-Wyllie...that would have been a lulu. Not to be missed. But, of course, neither happened nor threatened to happen.

I was conscious of the rumours of the fight and, later, the much more damaging one about the Fox-Whetton conspiracy against Buck but I ignored them. I felt that by responding to them I might, to some contorted minds, give them credibility and even leave myself open to charges that I was protesting too much. As far as I was concerned, if there was no truth in it, it couldn't harm me. That was a serious misjudgement.

Just to clarify our on-field relationship...basically as captain Buck gave me a free hand with the backs. If he wanted change he would give such directions as, "Get it close, put it in the air" and I would comply. But our tactics, by and large, were pre-planned and there was no question of Buck calling back moves. No forward I know of does that because it is impracticable. But if Buck thought our tactical approach, as opposed to calling moves, was not going as he wanted he would tell me to try something else.

I have said that when Buck was dropped for the Australian tests the same year I was surprised and that it was a matter between Buck and the selectors. There was the well-recorded business of Grizz referring to Buck's injury and of Buck's surprise that he should be judged to have any injury. It was, nevertheless, fairly well understood that Buck was carrying an injury – I think to the hip. It may not have been a seriously debilitating one but it was not news to everyone that it was there. It is no criticism of him that he was carrying an injury – plenty of us have done that!

Zinzan Brooke – suffered from the Bring Back Buck campaign,

– and it is truer of Buck than of any other player I know that he has an incredibly high pain threshold. In the third test against Australia in 1988 he was kicked in the head and badly gashed. He got up and played on like a dynamo. He was seemingly indestructible and he had my absolute admiration. Buck's a fighter and he would have undertaken to guts his way through pain barriers which would stop others stone dead. No ifs, no buts, no excuses, he'd have played.

When, after giving Buck the soft-option by saying he was dropped because of injury, it was stated his form was not up to his own high standards I related that immediately to an injury problem. Here, I will have a shot at second-guessing the selectors: We had been exposed defensively against Scotland through a lack of communication behind the backline. Tries had been scored because of defensive lapses which were uncharacteristic of the All Blacks. One of Buck's great strengths was going forward, getting the ball across the advantage line. Our shallow defensive cover had been well organised with the experienced players who were now gone and that had been a plus for Buck. Now it had been exposed. It was not his fault. We were not doing it well as a team. Zinny Brooke had been playing great rugby for Auckland and, within his overall competence, his covering defence was a feature. He had more speed than Buck and he was better than Buck going backward.

We were due to go into a test series against Australia and against one of the finest tactical kickers the game has known. Given our defensive difficulties against Scotland I suggest the selectors looked at Australia and the likely tactics and opted for Zinny's greater mobility. To my mind Buck was more the victim of the guys who were not now playing than of any other factor and that element was compounded by his injury. It may be forgotten that in 1989 the critics were on Buck's back before the tour of Wales and Ireland because he did seem to be struggling. Then, when the selectors named Gary Whetton vice-captain it was taken as a hint that if Buck's form did not come right he would be dropped, that his position was in jeopardy. In fact, that was quite wrong. They appointed a vice-captain because this was a long tour and they wanted someone to share the off-field load. The media got it wrong and the public got it wrong. Eventually, Buck had a storming tour, quite magnificent.

Over the whole Shelford saga I was sorry for two players – Zinzan, because he was not given his dues for winning test selection, and Gary, whose elevation to captain came after distinguished leadership of Auckland. All-consuming was eagerness to believe that Buck had been dealt-to by sinister means but at the heart of that was baseless rumour.

The rumour-machine had bolted and it was not to be caught. It grumbled through our comprehensive defeat of Australia in the first test, gained velocity with a less commanding win in the second and went rampantly nutty when we were snuffed out in the third. It gluttonised on the two regional defeats in France before we won the tests and then it took a deep breath through the summer and stretched to new idiocy in the winter of '91.

Everyone, but everyone, knew the "real story". Dustmen, lawyers, advertising clerks, share-brokers, ditch-diggers, drain-layers, doctors and nurses and even journalists...they all knew someone who knew someone who was a close friend of one of the All Blacks who was in the dressing-room or was party to the conspiracy against Buck.

At his table-tennis club my brother-in-law was approached by someone who knew the "real story". He described in vivid detail the Shelford-Fox fight in the dressing-room and confidently flew the conspiracy kite. My brother-in-law said it was interesting and perhaps the guy might like the opportunity of discussing it with me. You know Grant Fox? the guy asked. Well, yes, he's married to my sister. The retreat in confusion left Napoleon's in the shade.

When we were in Australia – and taking a beating at Sydney – Terry O'Connor, formerly of the *Daily Mail* and now writing for *The European*, and one of New Zealand's better friends among the English media, wrote a piece which yet again offered credibility to the whole Auckland conspiracy fabrication and my supposed part in it. His story was reprinted in at least one New Zealand daily newspaper. I was advised to take legal action but I considered that would create bad vibes for rugby. It had all become so outrageous. I was sickened by it as I watched my family suffering through it. After the test against Australia at Eden Park I asked Eddie Tonks, the chairman of the New Zealand Rugby Union, to do something about it and he made a statement. But it was not ended. Not by far. The lies had achieved such acceptance that denials were treated with cynicism, seen as some sort of cover-up. It was the stuff of nightmares.

After the World Cup match against Scotland at Cardiff I was walking to a bus with Bob Howitt, editor of New Zealand's *Rugby News*. I became aware that Terry O'Connor was alongside me. I rounded on him furiously and let rip with a few judgements of my own, something I had never done to a pressman before. Terry said, "Are you talking to me?" I said, "You bloody bet I am." And I told him the allegations were untrue, libelous. Had he spoken to any of the parties who were supposed to be involved? He said, "I had it on very good authority." Very good authority. That's a convenient piece of anonymity. It sounds impressive but it

Bruce Deans – another punch-up fantasy.

means precisely nothing. Certainly his "very good authority "
was a very authoritative liar. I cut loose again. Terry said, "I'm
sorry you feel that way." I can't imagine how he thought I should
have felt.

Hey. Did you hear the one about Fox and Deans?: You know,
about the punch-up. You know, about Bruce whacking Fox in
Christchurch. You know, because Fox was such a bastard to half-
backs and was responsible for Deans being dropped from the All
Blacks. Did you hear that one? Well, it's got to be true. Everyone,
just everyone, in Christchurch knows about it...

Oh hell. Here we go again. Let's get the ghost-busting over
and done with. Before the team was announced to play Wales on
the 1989 tour Grizz asked me to come into the selection meeting.
He told me he was thinking of playing Graeme Bachop instead of
Bruce and what did I think? It was the first time in my career as
an All Black I had been asked which half-back I preferred and I
was surprised. I said I did not have a preference and nor did I
want to be saddled with the responsibility of ending one player's

test career just as, equally, I did not want to be responsible for denying a new player a start in test rugby. I pointed out Bruce and I had played 10 tests together and had yet to lose one. Grizz thought Graeme, with a longer, faster pass would give a better start to the sort of rugby he wanted to play. I said, "You're the selector. You're the one who has to pick them", and left the room.

Grizz is a very sensitive man. He had intense loyalty to his players and he found it difficult to drop a player who had given him loyal service. He was considering dropping the player he knew better than anyone else in the team. I think he had already made up his mind and wanted support for his decision. The team was named with Graeme as half-back. We went to training and Bruce asked me if Grizz had talked to me. I told him exactly what had happened and he had no problems with it. I have not seen him often since the 1989 tour but once in Christchurch he said to me, "I was asked whether you and I had a fight and I said, 'Yeah, and I beat the shit out of him.' And he gave his wry grin.

Only twice in my career have I influenced selection and one of those occasions did involve a half-back. Late in 1989 Brett Iti was in danger of being dropped by the Auckland coaches, Maurice Trapp and Bryan Williams. They told me what they planned and I argued very strongly that we should retain Iti. They did. Brett did not know that and, probably, still doesn't. After he went to rugby league in Britain Auckland's *Sunday News* ran a back-page piece under some headline like "Fox Forced Me to go to Rugby League Says Iti". It was a small part of a long interview in an English newspaper. The following week there was a retraction of sorts inside the paper. It had Iti denying I had any major part in his decision to go to league.

What Brett didn't know was that I was his biggest ally. He came into the Auckland squad, an immensely talented, purely-instinctive player. I always asked new players to come to training early and we'd spend time together. Familiarisation, I guess. Brett couldn't believe all this organisation. He was a marvellous little runner, a try-a-game man, but not especially good at selecting the time to run. His passing was erratic and I spent a lot of time with him – as did Bryan Williams – and we called in the former All Black half-back Lin Colling to help. I did get frustrated sometimes during games and I may have been hard on him but he had so much talent I wanted to see his game coming together. I used to say to him, "You want to be an All Black? It's all about hard work, mate." I pointed to the example of Andy Haden who, at the age of 35, was always working at his lineout coordination with Sean Fitzpatrick.

By late 1989 it was all starting to work. Brett emerged from his shyness and told me he had a much bigger pass than I thought.

Brett Iti – the try-a-game man.

Would I stand wider? I would. And suddenly we had a great thing going. Now his instinct for the break was a huge asset because he was better able to select options.

The other occasion when I diverted selectors was, again, in 1989 when Auckland planned to drop Joe Stanley for a match against Waikato. My reaction was disbelief. I wanted Joe there and said so.

And there was, of course, the storm in a teacup between

Graham Lowe and me when I challenged Matthew Ridge to justify his claim that several young All Blacks were disillusioned with rugby union and that there would be substantial defections to league after the World Cup. Graham, for whom I have the greatest admiration, was called in to react to my reaction and took exception to something I said about his powers of media manipulation. It was meant as a compliment from one who is overwhelmed by the media-hype league is able to encourage through sensational marketing expertise. Graham suggested I must be upset because I had not been approached to play league. I am nothing if not a realist. I'd be bloody hopeless at league but that doesn't mar my enjoyment of it and I've never put it down as a game.

I hate rumour. I have seen one of my closest friends, Martin Crowe, taken to the cleaners by the most vicious allegations about his sexuality, culminating in the accusation that he is an Aids sufferer. Those rumours simmer along, helped on their way by nudges and winks from people who regard themselves as responsible citizens. No matter the public rejection of them by the "victims", damage has been done and some of the stigma sticks.

Ghost-busting may seem to be a tiresome business. But if you don't strike back with the truth some time, the phantoms will haunt away unchallenged and the families will go on suffering.

Probably the emptiest question I have been asked since the World Cup is whether the All Blacks would have won it had Buck Shelford been captain. Usually it has been asked by way of implying that had Buck been running the ship things would have been different. In some manner I'm sure things would have been different because Buck's style was different from Gary Whetton's. But to propose that Buck would have made the difference between winning and not winning against Australia is pie in the sky. There are too many unknown factors. For instance, would Buck's power to lead from the front – his greatest strength as a captain – have been a potent factor at the end of 1991? Accepting it was not a conspiracy but rather the judgement of three men, the selectors, that his form of 1990 was not good enough how could it be assumed he would have regained it more than a year later? Top fitness and form were essential to Buck's style of leadership.

It is unlikely that under Buck the game plan would have been any different. It is unlikely that under Buck we would have persuaded the Australians to change their game plan. But who knows? All is surmise. It is interesting, though, that the "deep significance" of captaincy has rarely been so aggressively analysed as since the Buck saga.

The captain has a total grasp of the game plan, oversees it, and if players in the shot-calling roles have not identified the need for change he calls for a new direction. A captain is not necessarily a good captain because he hounds his players along, walks up and down the lineout hammering his fist into the palm of his hand and shouting. When we speak of "great" captains like Wilson Whineray, like Brian Lochore and like Andy Dalton we speak of captains of presence, quiet men with the feeling for team performance and co-ordination, able to identify the need for change and institute it without fuss.

Buck was one of those captains who was seen to be marshalling the troops constantly. He was a talking captain, an urging captain, a demanding captain. It was his style. And built into that was his capacity, by compelling example, to urge the game onwards. That was Buck when playing at his quite awesome optimum. When tap-penalty moves and intricate wall-moves were called Buck would move among his troops yelling the code name, demonstrative, vocal.

Gary achieved as much in a different way. In the tap-penalty moves Gary was always in the wall. Buck never was. Gary communicated by hand signals and I would pass the word down the line. The objective was fulfilled. Given a penalty Buck would grab the ball and thrust it to me. Gary would walk by and say quietly, "Shoot it."

At a pause in the game Buck would be seen in the middle thumping the fist, voluble, demanding. Gary was more inclined to make a point and call on key players for input specific to their positions. Were judgement of captaincy to be made purely on results it would be true that Buck's years were more successful. Yet a study of team personnel would show that Buck's teams had the stamp of the 1987 World Cup on them. In fact, Buck put his finger on the difference when, writing in a British newspaper after we had been beaten by Australia, he said: "The fact is that the All Blacks have not been properly equipped to play the style of rugby they have been attempting in this tournament...there is nothing wrong with the philosophy of wanting to run with the ball but first you must have the players to carry out the plan."

Right on, Buck, right on. And that would have come from the heart because teams under Buck's captaincy, by and large, did have the equipment. As I have said already, our failing was in not more conservatively choosing our cloth to suit our pockets.

I am not interested in judging Buck and Gary to the detriment of one or the other. I do know, from having been in the middle of it with both, that in most respects one was as effective as the other but with different style. I would also say as confidently that captaincy was not the problem at the World Cup.

My first All Black captain was Jock Hobbs, the Christchurch lawyer, who gave his team that right royal bollocking at half-time in my first match in Fiji. It took me by surprise because he

Andy Dalton – one of a kind.

was such a studious-looking man, quietly spoken, gentle of manner off the field. I doubt there has ever been a captain of anything so committed to the team cause, tireless, laying his body on the line at the bottom of the rucks, always in thinking mode.

I have said that integrity lay at the root of the players' regard for Brian Lochore. I would say the same of Andy Dalton. As a diplomat, dealing quietly and, I might say, respectfully with the media he was one of a kind. I had little experience playing with him – he was struck out of the Cavaliers tour so early, belted on the jaw from behind by Burger Geldenhuys with as cowardly a blow as I have ever seen. That as clean a player as Andy should have been on the receiving end of it made it even more infamous. There was much of the old school in Andy – much the same devotion, I would imagine, as Whineray and Lochore gave to captaincy. As a short-end of the lineout player he had no equal in his time.

David Kirk inherited the captaincy from Andy. From the time he played a commanding role in the South Island's defeat of North in 1982 he was destined for big things in New Zealand rugby. He was strong on motivational team-talks and he was, as a university man of distinction, much given to the use of long words. Long, long words.Where, for instance, when pissed-off about an unforced knock-on, one of us less complicated chaps might say balls, Kirky would say testicles. In the dressing-room, having bamboozled us with his vocabulary he would look at Joe Stanley and ask if he would mind translating for the rest of the class. With a few pungent one-syllable words Joe, to Kirky's delight, would do just that. He became intense and emotional before big events and in the dressing-room before the 1987 quarter-final against Scotland he was moved to tears. He was an astute reader of rugby, a fine player and, in the context of the first

Andy Haden – could dominate a game like no other player.

World Cup, a stand-out off-field spokesman and figurehead for New Zealand.

Andy Haden, my Auckland captain for so long, was more in your Buck mould of skipper, very much the senior pro, quite demonstrative and a willing debater of referees' decisions. He was full of what I will call Hadenisms... "Fire in the belly, chaps, ice-cold in the brain", "Don't let doubt enter your mind, it might want to live there..." Given the occasion he could dominate the lineout – and the game – like no other player.

All these captains were graduates of the motivational school, more the smiting of the hand on the shoulder and the "Play up, play up, and play the game!" captains than the pre-match tactical analysts worrying whether everyone had their lines right.

Captaincy apart, out of the World Cup failure rumour of one sort or another was bound to emerge. Rumour breeds on failure. One was that the All Blacks were in two camps, not just divided, but bitterly so. If it were so I was unaware of it. I was not unaware of occasional internal dissidence but that has been there before when things have not been going swimmingly on the field. When people talk of divisions they should be conscious of such divisions as have occurred in some touring British Isles teams. They have been divisions which have threatened tours, so bitterly have players of one Home Country set themselves up against those of another over such issues as captaincy and team selection. There was nothing remotely approaching that sort of fracture in our party.

Observers might have identified groups who always played golf together, groups who always played cards together, groups who had their places on the bus but that has been so ever since All Black teams existed. Different interests do not create divisions. Division of the sort suggested would not have been

Walter Little on the thrust – a sniff of the future.

allowed to develop. Was it Hart groups and Wyllie groups? Auckland v The Rest? Oldies v Youngies? Speaking from the middle of the World Cup campaign I had no inkling of anything disruptive of that sort and, had there been, I would not have had any part of it.

Considering that what had been everyone's target and desire went down the drains of Lansdowne Road the cup campaign finished on a high note at Cardiff Arms. The team gave an animated performance against Scotland in a match both sides desperately wanted to win. It got all of us, even those who watched from the sideline, back on the winning track and it was a fillip anyone who had not been part of the campaign could never understand. Cardiff Arms had seemed an undesirable stop-over when we left Dublin. It became a celebration. For Walter Little to score that sort of try was a sniff of the future, just as it was for Jon Preston to play so well in a game of that magnitude. It was predictable that feedback from home was shock-horror that Walter had not been playing in the major games of the tournament. Yet during the home season there were those who were calling for his head. Walter will understand what I mean. I hope the young men of that team are able to enjoy the experience of winning the 1995 World Cup.

All that remained was to be a spectator at Twickenham. I do not spectate very well but this was something else. Steinlager invited Grizz, Alan Whetton and myself to be their guests for the day. The Ritz at 10am, don't you know, to meet some international corporate dignitaries, then to float on champagne bubbles to Twickers in what was the yuppy bus to end them all – one and a-half hours of champers, Steinie, lobster, caviar, pheasant. This was a bus? Definitely a tip or two there for the Auckland Regional Council.

At Twickers the Scots team greeted us wearing Aussie hats and scarves. Very pointed, we thought. Up in the corporate box we were treated as, and behaved as close as we could get to, royalty. Prince Grizz and I went out to the balcony to chat about private jets and palaces and someone hollered out to us from the next box. Hollered, I tell you. Dame Kiri Te Kanawa, prima donna assoluta, hollered! She and her husband and children came over to our box for a spot and a yarn. I was in awe of this lady but she was one of us, talking Grizz and Foxy language to the manner born.

When the band played the national anthem a hilarious clan of Scots just in front of us sang Flower 'o Scotland lustily but very badly and the game was on. It was the oddest sensation...Twickers, the World Cup final, roaring crowds and not a black jersey in sight.

10

The reluctant twins

A t the World Cup of 1991 the All Blacks had the two best coaches in New Zealand. But one of them would have been better. Either one. This twin-coach system, thrust embarrassingly on to two men neither of whom wanted it, was never going to work. It would become an encumbrance. It would create discomfort for the coaches and for the players. It was an act of folly to place Grizz Wyllie and John Hart in tandem virtually at the countdown to the All Blacks' participation in rugby's greatest showpiece.

John Hart did not want to go to the World Cup. His perception was that the team was struggling and that on the evidence of its difficulties against Scotland and Australia it was unrealistic to expect it to be transformed into the dashing performer of '87-88-89. If the team succeeded the honour would be Grizz's as the incumbent coach and, should he pursue it, a further term would be his for the asking. If it failed Hart would be seen to have failed with it. To promote himself John had to stay at home. Catch 22. If he stayed at home he would be seen to lack patriotism at a time when the New Zealand Rugby Union clearly judged the on-field game to be in crisis and that would be an end, anyway, to the achievement of his desired goal – the coaching of the All Blacks in his own time.

So, against his better judgement, he undertook the assignment and with it the renewal of a relationship which was known to be as fragile as eggshells, the approach to coaching of the two men as disparate as the personalities of the men themselves. Nominally, at least, Grizz had the predominant role. In the actuality they were cast in roles of equality. Running the team day-about had all the ingredients to cook up confusion. And the obvious thing to the players was that Grizz knew it wasn't working and John knew it wasn't working.We were a boat with two helmsmen, each one with the same home port but each one steering his own course. At team talks there was general discomfort when, instead of nominating Grizz to deliver the final word, the manager, John Sturgeon, threw it at the pair of them to sort out on the spot.

After the World Cup when Grizz, angered by official criticism of him (leaked to the media), withdrew his candidacy for the new panel the NZRFU selection committee of seven recommended Hart. Even though it was known that John's articulate self-confidence got on the administration's wick it did not seem possible that then the full council, with one cavalier flourish, could dispose of him against the recommendation of its appointed committee. Ostensibly, he was moved along on the basis of the one loss he had sustained in all the matches in which he had had a coaching involvement with New Zealand teams – the Dublin loss to Australia. I say ostensibly because it would be naive to suppose there was not some undercurrent of personality conflict. The New Zealand Rugby Union had, in effect, required him to go to the World Cup. Now the New Zealand Rugby Union was saying that was an error of judgement. As if Hart did not know that before the event! And Grizz, too.

So John Hart was the ultimate loser from the World Cup. Grizz had had his time as coach and a triumph it had been. The players, or most of them, would live to fight another day, another winter. But where the future for a man like Hart? He does not even have the opportunity to fashion the future of his brilliant young players from the Colts and that is a tragedy for rugby.

That is not a criticism of the new panel. It is not their fault John Hart was rejected. It is my greatest hope they, with their players, can restore New Zealand rugby to pre-eminence. But it is a criticism of a process which can deny a distinguished coaching record even exists.

When the All Blacks went to Japan after the 1987 World Cup it was with Hart as coach, assisted by Wyllie. That was seen by the players to be a sign of things to come. Not so. Later Russ Thomas, then chairman of the NZRFU, using the quaint logic of convenience, denied Hart had ever been dropped as All Black coach because the Japan matches were not "cap" tests. It was pedantry flirting with the bizarre. We had been selected as All Blacks, we felt as All Blacks, we played as All Blacks in full All Black kit and we were in Japan as winners of the World Cup.

There was a narrow-minded notion in New Zealand that rugby players were divided into two distinct categories. There were the Wyllie men and there were the Hart men. The Hart men

Fragile triumverate – Wyllie, Sturgeon and Hart after Hart had been called in for the Australian test at Eden Park in 1991.

were adamantly opposed to Wyllie as were the Wyllie men to Hart. It was a notion which thrust its narrow-mindedness on the players as if they were incapable of rational thought on the matter. It will be clear now that I have strong views on the elimination of Hart from top-level coaching but I never regretted my All Black career with Wyllie. Here he was, we supposed, this rough, tough bugger with red-and-black eyeballs, straining at the leash to put us through his gut-busting training runs. Preconceptions are notoriously frail. Grizz was no charmer, just a gruff straight-shooter, basically shy till you were accepted, a man who needed the company of men for whom he had respect and who respected him. And, if I may extend the psycho-analysis into something more tangible: he was, in his singular way, a hell of a rugby coach.

Different coaches, different means. I am not a great believer in "inspirational" team-talks. I know there have been coaches whose passionate pleas to the players have taken in queen and country, bloody battlefields, the families back home, the cows waiting to be milked, the sheep to be shorn, the green and pleasant land, the state of the nation, the rugby union's destitution and now for God's sake get out there and kill those bastards for everyone back home.

Motivation comes from the individual. If it is not in the player to motivate himself, if he has not prepared himself mentally for what is to come, an "inspirational" team-talk is not going to make the difference. Preparation is the vital ingredient. Some players, a few, have the innate ability to switch on, to become at the flick of a mental switch intensely focussed on the game and on the requirements on them. But for most it is an installed confidence that the days of training, the days of thinking about the opposition have prepared them to handle whatever contingency the game throws up.

There is some graphic evidence that French forwards, and especially props and hookers, bloody themselves up for the fray by nose-butting the dressing-room walls. Very Gallic and not to be recommended to the old college first XV. It is alleged by old All Blacks that some South African hinterland forwards prepare themselves for the one big match of their lives by having themselves locked in a cage for a month with a man-eating lion and a haunch or two of raw kudu to battle over, get themselves released, ravenous, on match day and charge out to top-up on raw New Zealander. There may be some slight exaggeration in this but undoubtedly some Boer farmers of staggering physical proportions and mean appetites have made their impact on touring All Blacks.

Those exceptions apart, there is much to be said for a calm preparation. If the right things have not been said and done in the longer build-up the last team-talk is not going to make a difference. All the coaches I have been involved with have their own ways, their own strengths.

John Hart and Grizz were poles apart. Harty brought all the elements of artful persuasion, pinpricking a bit here, flattering a bit there, demanding more from this prop, reminding the wing that tries do not grow on trees for the plucking, drilling this first five-eighths with a reminder that automation has no part in the game plan, changing the pitch of his voice from appeal to demand, reflecting on the family at home watching on television, using body-language to emphasise a point, picking his marks astutely but always coming back to team performance. He was a student of the individual and in the days leading up to a match he would quietly make his points one-on-one. More complex than Grizz.

Grizz kept his team-talks short and direct. No bullshit. His team-talks were what Grizz was and what he had been as a player. No room for fastidious analysis from individual to individual. "Fastidious? Don't give me that poncey crap." No shades of grey. Black and white. And red. Red for a sort of built-in anger simmering away barely below the surface. Grizz had played the game like an angry man. Oratory? "Don't give me that bullshit." But, yes. Oratory of a rugged, rough-hewn sort. Compelling, too.

But his mannerisms told you he felt this dressing-room stuff was not really his gig. He needed his boots on and the ball in his hands out there on the paddock calling the shots.

From his experience as a player for Canterbury and New Zealand he could sense the need at times for unusual remedies. In 1988 after we had snatched a 19-19 draw with the Wallabies at Brisbane he gave us a pretty powerful serve and told us to make sure we packed our training gear on top of our bags. Grizz looked and sounded mean, man, real mean. We flew to Sydney, drove to the Eastwood Club for training and feared the very worst. Grizz glowered, "Get your gear, get into the dressing room and get changed." We were in various stages of undress when Grizz said, "Forget it. We're having a piss-up." I started to get out my gear and into my clothes. Warwick Taylor muttered, "Leave it on, Foxy, leave it on. It's going to be one of those days." As a Canterbury man, Warwick knew Grizz through and through. It was, indeed, one of those days. It's hard on a young chap from Auckland when a monster like Grizz sets the pace and gets very, very suspicious, not to say belligerent, if you don't keep up. Much later we fell off the bus and into the arms of an understanding press corps. Grizz had planned the whole show. Win, lose or draw it was going to happen.

We went on that tour riding high on our defeats of Wales at home. But suddenly Grizz changed our training methods. He introduced training without the ball and it became a frustration for everyone. He abolished the up-and-under as an attacking weapon except in extreme circumstances – like desperation. We were winning our lead-up games to the first test, but not with a lot of satisfaction. We were wearing criticism because of the level of performance. The guys were getting edgy. So Grizz called a shit session before the first test. Let it all out, he said. Everyone had a say and, me being me, I probably said more than most. Most of the comment was critical of our training methods. Grizz nodded a lot but said little. He released the balls for our training warm-ups. Then he said, "Get into the up-and-unders."

Cunning. Some might call it low, animal cunning. Grizz had sensed the boys were getting a bit cocky after so comfortably handling Wales. He was going to knock that particular crap out of us. He was prepared to wear a bad press because he knew the Aussies would be reading it, too, and he was prepared to constrict our performance to that end. It was no secret the Wallabies were less difficult to beat when they were overly confident. So he orchestrated the whole thing and we walloped the Wallabies, using the up-and-under to great effect. Grizz was always prepared to take criticism from tour matches as he worked toward winning the tests.

Brian Lochore – felt fiercely the honour of representing New Zealand. Here he is with the rest of the panel which sent me to Fiji, Bryce Rope, left, and Tiny Hill.

Grizz had a great knowledge of the game. It was not always easy for him to project verbally everything he was carrying in his head. He cared. Above all, he cared. He cared for the players and he wanted to be part of the camaraderie of touring. Once relaxed, he had a vast appetite for his own robust – some who have felt it might say bellicose – kind of give-and-take sociability, with a sharing of good booze, a swapping of outrageous insults, and a whack or two around the ears.

After my first tour, to Fiji under Bryce Rope, I came into the Lochore coaching era. Brian exuded this aura of deep integrity and it was this, perhaps more than any other quality, which drew players to him. He felt fiercely the honour of playing for one's country, had felt it as a player, felt it as a coach and expected it from his players. He was motivational in his team-talks yet self-possessed and controlled, but the nearer the test came the more you could sense BJ becoming involved in the excitement of it, like a man who would be playing the test himself. He was an active coach, saturated in the knowledge of his years as an All Black and as a great All Black captain. He was a planner for the occasion and a stickler for having "a couple of moves" up our sleeve. No more than a couple. But a couple of perfection. Look, he used to say, we don't want and we don't need all these bloody Flash Harry moves. They get in the way and they'll get us into trouble. As a Wairarapa farmer he regarded with disdain players who suffered, as he put it, from sleeping sickness, the guys who

Pinetree, the humble legend, delivers a charge.

lounged around in their hotel rooms watching Conan the Barbarian when outside there was all this fresh air. It was his rustic requirement for fresh air in preference to Conan which puzzled some players who protested they drew inspiration and motivation from the Barbarian whereas fresh air did nothing for them at all.

It was Lochore who identified the players' need for a spell away from the restless, noisy hype of hotel-living during the 1987 World Cup. After we had played Fiji in Christchurch and before playing Argentina in Wellington he organised a break over in his own stamping ground at Pirinoa in the Wairarapa. We stayed there billetted with wonderful people for a day and a night, avoided Conan like the plague, cleansed our lungs with Lochore's fresh air, ate farm-style home-cooking and went to Wellington ready for anything.

I have referred to the use Lochore made of Grizz and John Hart during the 1987 campaign. It was a master-stroke that he could so successfully draw the two of them into the team-building process so that here was a panel of three harnessing their considerable skill to a common end.

There was something of both Lochore and Wyllie in Colin Meads, coach of the North Island and the Cavaliers. He shared with Grizz and BJ the man-of-the-land straightforward, no-frills simplicity. For a living legend he was just about the humblest man I ever met. When he studied you from below the forbidding eyebrows and over the formidable nose you felt somehow skewered. He kindled unswerving loyalty in his players and they knew that if they did not perform he could use the training paddock like an army bull-ring. As a player he had been part of the great era under Fred Allen and he had taken aboard many of the traits of his coach. Not the least of these was a demand for errorless routines on the training paddock. He hammered the point, as I have been told Fred did, that you pay a high price for mistakes in rugby and the beginning of mistakes in a match is mistakes on the training field. He had, too, the charming philosophy that what you stuffed or poured into your bodies you then balanced that enjoyment against an equivalent amount of pain to get rid of it. He knew South African rugby well, having toured the country in 1960 and 1970 and having played against the touring Springboks in 1965. To beat the South Africans in their own country demanded certain disciplines. He would hammer certain points home and then say, "Look. If you don't do it, you'll be sucking on the hind tit" and none of us relished that prospect.

Ian Kirkpatrick – fired a missile.

Odd that, like Grizz, he knew the way to a rugby player's heart. After Transvaal had beaten the Cavaliers we went to Cape Town to play Western Province and we were smarting. We had not, after all, gone to South Africa to lose anything. We had a team meeting at which Pinetree slagged us. A humbling experience, that. Then Ian Kirkpatrick – another bloody farmer – delivered a low-flying missile and Andy Dalton, a country yokel from way back, beat us over the head with a hay-baler. You might call our state of mind subdued as we prepared for a ripper of a training run. Pinetree stretched, stared at the ceiling and said quietly, thoughtfully, "One of the problems with this team is that you don't drink enough good booze. Before training we'll drink a beer to a time to be called by Robbie Deans." Three hours later we were still talking mostly in fluent Urdu and two days later we went out and blew Western Province away for 40 minutes and still had enough left to win comfortably at the end of 80.

Whatever your viewpoint on the advisability, or even the morality, of the Cavaliers tour you may care to judge people like Pinetree Meads and Ian Kirkpatrick on what they have given to New Zealand and world rugby. I submit it outstrips by a country mile any hindrance to rugby their participation in that tour may be judged to have caused.

Trapp and Williams – the meticulous and the dynamic.

An interesting pair of coaches, Maurice Trapp and Bryan Williams. A pom, albeit a long-serving Kiwi pom, tall, with the look of a scholar and built like a geometrical quiz question...identify the 56 different angles in this diagram. A New Zealand-born Samoan, built like a mobile totara trunk with muscles and a law degree – and a rugby career studded with more honours than an American five-star general (if they go to five stars). Maurice and Bryan had a hard act to follow, the Hart act, as they sought continuation of Auckland's dominating influence on New Zealand provincial rugby. Maurice was a meticulous student of the game. He took more notes on any one game than a university student in a year of lectures. He was strongly into the tactical reading of the game and as a long-serving lock in the Auckland scrum he knew forward play intimately. He was coaching's quiet man, diligent, alert to motivational opportunities and highly respected by the players.

Bryan was more inclined to appeal to the emotions, drilling home the excitement of the occasion, using his own experience to illustrate his points. Probably there was more of the Hart approach here. As a player who had been named in 1980 as the Player of the Decade he would not see individual flair suffocated. In a world where it may seem sometimes that individual expressiveness is so subservient to team patterns and disciplines that it is rugby's threatened species, he encouraged players to insinuate their brilliance into the game.

Last year I read somewhere that an unnamed Auckland club coach was niggling away with the allegation that Trapp and Williams were the Auckland coaches in name only, that the team was being coached by Gary Whetton and myself and that our lack of interest in doing other than enough to win was the cause of the team's boring displays. The beginning of another rumour? We did not coach the team but were happy to have an input when consulted by the coaches – just as they consulted Fitzpatrick or McDowell on front row problems. It would be an unusual, a self-defeating, situation were coaches not to discuss rugby with their senior players. To suggest we had lost the spark to animate the team and, in effect, that we deliberately put the brakes on it is simply not true. I would add that rugby teams, no matter how good they are, cannot week after week, year after year, turn in performances to exhilarate the crowds. The demands on the top players beyond their heavy provincial commitments – and especially with a team holding the Ranfurly Shield – are such that there are bound to be matches when their performance drifts away. I am as proud of playing for Auckland now as I was as a youngster. I would be happy to tell that anonymous club coach all about it.

11

The way we are

Not to put too fine a point on it, I can be a little prick on the rugby field. It has something to do with my demands on myself, something with my demands on others. In a way the two are inextricable. It has much to do with my acceptance of the ultimate responsibility of having the backs run smoothly, of calling the shots. I need that responsibility. I play my best rugby when I have it. I am intense by nature. I react with volatility. I talk vehemently at myself and I talk vehemently at other players. Sometimes I have been too demanding, especially on young players. But when you see me spit my mouthguard and deliver a few well-chosen words I promise you, it's not all bad.

To players who know me well, who play most of their rugby with me, that side of me is quite the dressing-room joke. Foxy played one of his best mouths today. Laughs all round. Me too, I have laughed about it with the Whettons, Fitzy, Joe Stanley and JK, Johnny the Schu and if I've had a bit of a go at one of the young guys I talk to him about it afterward, work it out. That marvellous referee the late Kerry Fitzgerald couldn't believe me in Japan in 1987. Here was this little guy going loudly nuts, yelling abuse. It was me abusing me. Kerry looked at me very dubiously, raised his eyebrows, shook his head and went back to Australia to dine out on it. Maybe I'm some sort of masochist in search of chastisement.

Odd that in 1991 I should be hit with the most constant criticism of my demanding, yapping ways on the field at a time when I was having far less of that sort of influence on the game. I was approached by players and coaches and asked to wind down. It was done fairly and squarely and with the best of intentions. There were concerns about my relationships with

Playing one of my best mouths – giving JK ammunition for some dressing-room banter.

others, particularly the younger players in the team. Some may have thought I had too much to say, too much responsibility. No one previously had made any such approach. The coaches could see I was struggling a little and, knowing my intensity, they related that to its effect on others. As a player I did not think cutting back on my responsibilities was good for my game because I fed on that requirement. Had I sensed the problem I would have called the guys together myself to get it out into the open. The outcome was that when I was getting considerable media hounding about the influences I exerted on the field those influences had actually decreased dramatically.

My attitudes to other players are dictated by the rules I play to myself. When I see quite exceptional natural talent being squandered because natural talent is seen to be enough I can become decidedly abrupt. Talented players become great players when they work at it, not by divine right. I'm the guy who had to slog away for hours to make something more of average ability and I see players of much more natural ability than I sitting back on their talent as if that is all it needs. It is as if they do not really want to become better players.

I was always as likely to give Gary Whetton a burst as I was Craig Innes but I did not often enough make allowances for the sensitivity of young players. I used to tell players like Craig Innes and Walter Little to let it roll off their backs. But what I really meant was "don't ignore what I'm trying to do for you; just ignore the way I do it." Where I had feed-back from senior players like Schuster and Stanley here I was getting none – which was just an added frustration. Had, say, Craig been able to bring himself to say, "Gotcha, Foxy. Now shut up" or had Walter bounced a few back, maybe had the confidence to say, "You buggered that up, Foxy. Pull yourself together. Concentrate" I'd have died happy.

When I think back on it all I realise I was just that intense when I played footy as a kid. I couldn't run as fast as others and, really, my physique was thrown together by someone who had never heard of rugby or, having heard of it, decided it was not the game for me. So how could I enjoy it? By working so I could do some things better than the others. Probably I take more satisfaction, more enjoyment, out of rugby than most international players because everything I have achieved is the result of working to overcome my natural disadvantages. It may look on those television close-ups as if it's all a pain in the arse but I promise you I am enjoying myself out there. And I'm enjoying myself best when we win.

The All Blacks have a saying, "Better never to have been an All Black than to have been a bad All Black." The histories are littered with the names of players who got there and then copped out. There's a pub game which searches the memory for the names of players who slipped into the All Blacks for one game, maybe two. The commonest phraseology as the next pint goes down is, "Yeah. Him. Forgot about him. What a loser." The poor guys are held in contempt; no kudos for having been very good provincial players, just contempt for being eminently forgettable All Blacks. The players who get there have a built-in demand on themselves not to be the next pub-game loser. The best All Blacks are those who have to work to get there and, having got there, work to stay there. Getting to the top is easy compared with staying there. Each year I've worked that little bit harder, that little more intensely at my skills. A year older is three years more difficult to get fit.

One reason so many of us are so sensitive to criticism is that there is little understanding out there how much sweat, graft and pain go into being an All Black. Yet no player I know resents that, because at the end of it the reward of playing a top game overcomes all. Exhaustion after a hard-won victory is a sweet pain. After my first test, against Argentina, Brian Lochore asked me how I felt. Never before had I felt so deeply, so bone-achingly weary, so mentally stuffed. But I told him I felt great. Just great. And meant it from the heart.

I would rather by far have been at the top for a long time and suffer from the tall poppy syndrome than play well only occasionally and be lavishly lauded for it.

I have said that the Carling analysis of the New Zealand rugby "professional" is so wide of the mark it is out of the ball park. There is a commercial side to rugby these days – as no one knows better than Will – which brings in an erratic supplementary income, but only for some. No one here that I know is in rugby for the money. There are the very few from most countries who are able to play rugby the year around but that is a short-lived "career". Like most of the fortunate people who have jobs, we have to protect them because the days are long gone when an All Black on the staff was a matter of pride or a public relations gimmick worth all the absences. There is no place on staffs these days for unproductive workers.

That figurehead status no longer applies.

We use the word professional about our attitude to playing the game not about our bank balances. We give to rugby what we can while first devoting our time to our families and our jobs. Rugby is not the most dominant thing in our lives yet, in a way, it dominates our lives.

After the World Cup John Hart commented that he thought the All Blacks had their minds on other things, commercial things. We agreed as a team before the tournament that we would minimise commercial activities for the duration. The feeling was that there would be commercial spin-off to be gained by winning the trophy, not by getting to the final. The Australians were really active commercially and for them it paid off. What, in fact, Hart was saying was that we were being asked to perform to the ultimate in playing professionalism, to give the game the time to that end while being weighed down with the responsibility also of making a living – that, in effect, we were becoming addicted to the need for sustenance. It was a warning to the game's administration that this sort of pressure cannot go on without a change of policy.

The All Blacks have been called many things by the media. The favoured description is "the unsmiling giants" and variations on the theme. Well, I suppose the public face of the All Blacks is a bit like that. Much of it, especially close to match days, is the realisation that a large part of our country is concerned not only that we play well but that we win. For the players there is euphoria after a test well won but often the first emotion is relief. And after a loss – an experience I have had three times in 35 tests up till the end of the second World Cup – you ask why you put yourself through it. But I doubt whether the players of any other country enjoy themselves among themselves on tour as we do. Everyone in his own way is a comedian, and if not a practising comedian then one, like myself, who laughs along to keep the others performing. Alan Whetton is a bottomless pit of one-liners. Richard Loe a story-teller who, in the best traditions of comedy, doesn't know how funny he is. The Schuler-Loe sheep-herding farce in Ireland was much more the All Black face I know on tour than the introverted grimness the public may perceive. The young guys are always playing world championships. World championships in anything bizarre that comes to mind. At this very moment Graeme Bachop is world champion at spinning a rugby ball on the tip of his finger while eating a soft-boiled egg with the other hand while reciting excerpts from The Iliad while dancing the lambada.

What the All Blacks consider to be fun does not involve throwing pies and buns around dining rooms. That's for the pub-school comedians of the other side of the world.

And why don't we hug and kiss and go down on our knees in front of the adoring fans when we score a try? Why this solemn acceptance of a try as if we have just completed an objectionable chore, like cleaning out a backblocks privy and there are still more to be done? It has ever been so. Even Wilson Whineray, as

It isn't all grim stoicism. The emotion hangs out in the dressing-room and here David Kirk seems to have something to be deliriously happy about.

far as can be judged on black and white film, didn't exactly burst into a paroxysm of delight when he scored that unworldly try against the Barbarians at Cardiff Arms. And Colin Meads didn't exactly plant a slushy kiss on his cheek did he? About the only time I can remember seeing an All Black from way back showing emotion after scoring a try was in film of the 1956 Springbok tour when the New Zealand lock Tiny White did a high-flying heel-kick. Surprisingly, he was not ex-communicated.

I think we're starting to come around to the realisation that scoring a try is not an occasion for macho stoicism. Remember Richard Loe scoring under half-a-ton of sweaty bodies, seeking out the cameras and giving that grotesque grimace which he alleged afterwards was his normal smile? Maybe had we reached the stage of professionalism that every try meant a $10,000 bonus to the team Richard would have been smothered with kisses with Stevie McDowell leading the charge.

I am sure New Zealand sports people are deterred from showing what they really feel because any emotional gesture is seen by the public to be woofterish, pretentious and intolerable. What is acceptable from the athletes of any other country is not acceptable from our own. Remember Rod Dixon, having won the New York marathon of 1983, going down on his knees and kissing the bitumen? It was an emotional expression of over-whelming elation. And why not? It was an immense achievement for which he had trained his body and mind to a razor's edge. But at home he got a bagging for it.

I am not by nature a demonstrative person but, may God forgive me, at Nantes in 1990 when we had beaten the French, I hugged Alan Whetton. I do not lie. He may have hugged me back. Should I recant?

I must say I'm not a barrelful of laughs in the days leading up to a test match. As the days go by I become more and more focussed on the game. If it is a home test my wife treats me like some fragile objet d'art and the children regard me with puzzlement. I'm some other guy. Remote. With the team, come match day, I'm left pretty much to myself. I'm not angry or aggressive. I just won't have my concentration broken. JK worries about being too intense. He uses music to relax to. He has a passion for saxophone and plays one himself. I do hope he improves quickly.

So what am I as a player? What is this critter called a first five-eighths? I played poorly in the three test losses the All Blacks had in that long era. After losses you have doubts about yourself. Are you really good enough to be there? I get no satisfaction out of personally playing well during a loss in any match. The game is all about team and if you do not embrace that you should not be playing it. I would like to think I am picked as a first five-eighths

Play it again, JK, you can only improve.

who can kick goals rather than a goal-kicker who can play first five-eighths. There are plenty who would debate that with me. Kicking goals is a string to the bow. It's like Sean Fitzpatrick, selected as a hooker, putting the ball on the button at the lineout. It's Graeme Bachop, selected as a half-back, getting it right with the hooker. The first five-eighths dictates play to the extent the tight five dictate play. The platform they set up determines what sort of ball is released and that determines the process in the backline. It also determines whether the loose forwards also have a platform to work off so the backs may be given ball going forward. That is paramount. If the first five-eighths receives the ball going forward he will, almost always, move it along as a wide-running option. If the ball is impeded or delayed at second phase the opposition has time to manoeuvre its defences so the first five-eighth looks for other options – the kick for position, the high kick, generally choosing to keep the ball close to set up another target for the forwards to run to.

The tight fives I have played with are conscious of their huge responsibility to the team performance and they revel in it. If they are not operating to that end the loosies are drawn into the tight, continuity is hard to establish and the plan breaks down. The bruisers, the rhinos...call them what you will, they make or break. At the same time the halfback and the first five-eighths – and in some measure the No 8 – have a responsibility to the tight five. The tactics we have used more recently have not helped. They have been too ambitious too early rather than setting foundations. In the past year, maybe two, I doubt that those responsible for bringing the tight five into the game-plan early have been sufficiently diligent in pursuing it.

There was some criticism at the World Cup that our big men were not attacking our own kick-offs and drop-outs, something which had been a trademark of New Zealand rugby in that we were re-establishing attacking positions with the ball in hand immediately on the resumption of play. Other teams have picked up on its value. The Australians always used to kick long but now they kick short searching for giants like Eales and McCall. More and more our own big men, Gary Whetton and Ian Jones, have found it difficult to navigate a path through opposition forwards placed in brick-wall obstruction. We tried to overcome this by having several different kick-offs, looking for the space so our followers could get a clear run at the ball. I believe we "over-technified". Better to have put the ball up there and fought for it than seeking the space.

Obviously, a major component of the five-eighths arsenal is the selection of options. While it is only comparatively recently that rugby audiences have latched on to the options market I am

Kicking with the "other" foot – adequacy is just acceptable.

far from being its pioneer.

Options are born from the tactics you take on to the field. They are part of applying the plan the team has discussed. I am offering the first option but always with the flexibility that if another team member thinks there is a better one in the circumstance of the game he will throw it into the ring.

Ideally, given perfection, a first five-eighths will kick accurately with either foot. Very few, perhaps none, kick sufficiently well with their "other foot". I have not done as much work with my left foot as I should have and it has deteriorated. Lynagh rarely uses his left foot, Camberabero may never have used it and Porta likewise. We would plan to force Lynagh on to his weak foot, thus cutting back his time. This did not involve only me as first five-eighths or the half-back or the loosies running at him more quickly. It involved, too, getting the tight five going forward to create pressure so his ball was rough.

The disadvantage of not having two good feet is that you

telegraph your intentions, make it easier for the opposition to second-guess where you will kick. For example: You receive the ball from a scrum on the right side of the field – that is, the half-back passing to his left. If you are going to box-kick or up-and-under you have to stop to do it. But if you have a left foot you can run a feint then kick back into the box.

To have no ability at all with the "wrong" foot is not to be contemplated. Adequacy is just acceptable.

A first five-eighths must be able to pass equally well off either hand, though he will have a favoured hand especially when throwing cut-out passes, which have become the rule rather than the exception. With modern defensive patterns it is almost impossible to move the ball through the hands of each back and have the try scored by the winger in the corner. It is very difficult to score tries from set pieces for the same reason. We try to keep the attack square so the cut-out pass is essential, while setting up diversions to keep the opposition in. We play a numbers game: create your target, play to hold the opposition loose forwards in and commit one or more of their backs at second-phase. So you have more players on attack than they on defence.

I have never had my freedom to run restricted by coaches or captains. It is simply not one of my strengths. I cannot accelerate like the brilliant young Otago player Marc Ellis. What I would have given for his legs! If I run there's a gap you could drive a team of oxen through. If I run I want a significant gain for the team. Between 1987 and 1991 we scored a lot of tries out wide. I take my satisfaction from nominating the move we score from and that is the continuing challenge for me. Few teams plan target moves involving the first five-eighths carrying the ball up. The French did when Franck Mesnel was at first five-eighths and when that tough little tank Philippe Rouge-Thomas was here in 1989, but essentially the first five-eighths is a player who runs given an opening. It may happen not at all, or once, perhaps twice, in a game and, ideally, every time he runs points result.

I have been accused of running less – and sometimes not at all – in recent times. I do not believe in taking on opposition teams for the sake of it. Probably I have been guilty of not looking for running opportunities – that, rather, my style has been to sit back and wait for them. It is also true that running opportunities for first five-eighths have been more intensively monitored than ever before.

Drop-kicking for goal is a five-eighths option much more favoured by northern than southern hemisphere teams. Down here we back ourselves to cross the try-line from the sort of attacking situation which sets up the drop-kick. For me, it is a tactic for a crisis, a game-breaker.

12

Five-eighths fantasy

For all my ambition, for all the need I placed on myself to become an All Black, I might never have made it had a first five-eighths named Nicky Allen had the orthodoxy of mind to be a long-termer rather than a nomadic adventurer. I have set down what are, to my mind, the essential ingredients of the first five-eighths game. Nicky had the sort of talent which, if not rewriting that particular text-book, would have added a chapter to it. Everyone who loves to see beauty in rugby, skills almost ethereal, far removed from the skills of mathematical precision, should by divine right have had the opportunity to watch Nicky Allen playing at first five-eighths. Nicky was everything to everyone. There seemed nothing he could not do better than anyone else, with the possible exception of kicking with his "wrong" foot, which happened to be his right. But I wouldn't even swear to that because Nicky might well have just been keeping his right foot under wraps, an emergency foot, lest his ubiquitous left dropped off.

He was at Auckland Grammar with me though senior to me. I remember him well because he stood out from the crowd, not in a bumptious way but because even at school he was a character from another world, living life as if there were no tomorrow and, to be sure, there were less tomorrows for Nicky than for most of us. He was the first XI left-arm quick bowler, in the senior basketball team and a stand-out in the first XV. He was to become an All Black in 1980 and to play such rugby in Wales that he moved Welshmen (who, better than any other living creatures, know a good fly-half when they see one) to tears. One of those emotionally moved by Nicky was Barry John who took him aside to a quiet corner and said, "Nicky, you have such glorious skills,

Nicky Allen, the ephemeral genius, backed by his captain, Graham Mourie.

but you have only one foot. You must work at the other one because you will need it." Nicky considered this while looking at one foot then the other. Then he nodded and said, "Barry, I think you're right. I will work at it. In the meantime I think one will be enough to beat Wales."

He had moved out of Auckland when I went into John Hart's team for the first time and when he returned we had a brief playing relationship with Nicky at second five-eighths. One day at Eden Park, I think in 1983, I watched him at training. He went to the corner of the 22-metre line on the right side of the field and drop-kicked a goal with his left foot. He went to the 22 on the left side of the field and drop-kicked a goal with his right. Then he went to the middle of the 22, turned his back on the posts and drop-kicked a goal with his heel. I pondered my future.

There was nothing Nicky could not do with a rugby ball. The story is already well told by the players who were there of his exchange with the All Black coach Eric Watson in Wales in 1980 when, as Watson expounded the game-plan, Nicky rhythmically bounced a ball off every natural bodily projection – and some which, by contortion, he manufactured. Watson gimlet-eyed him and demanded to know if he was listening. Nicky bounced on while reciting monotone every word the coach had said.

Nicky could step off either foot, wraith through a half-gap, had several eyes strategically placed around his head where most first five-eighths have only the usual two in front. He could run, he could pass and his left foot had a tertiary education. He also had a concussion problem and he knew any game might be his last. He was playing a club match in Australia when the tackle came which ended his rugby and his life.

I go on about Nicky because he, more than any other player I have known, showed that rugby is not only a matter of pre-ordained chess moves. Rugby needs Nicky Allens to uplift its spirits when it threatens to become too static a game. If in praising him I pinpoint my own limitations, so be it.

Perhaps had he stayed with us he would have found too little in the modern game to entertain him, too many disciplines, too much uniformity... "Hey, Foxy, too heavy, man."

I could see something of Nicky in Steve Pokere. Steve's father played with mine in the old Okato days and I am told he, too, was a beautifully balanced player. Steve suffered from his own versatility. He became that sort of wilderness player, a centre, a second five-eighths, a first five-eighths to be picked up and put down at the selectors' whim in whatever position.

Hugo Porta, my first international opponent, almost single-handedly, brought Argentine rugby out on to the international stage. He was everything to Argentina, tactician, an astute kicker in field play, a creator of play, a runner who could make something out of nothing by doing what he was not, sensibly, supposed to do. And he could kick goals in his sleep – not least of all drop-kick goals at which he was an acknowledged master and notably so against the All Blacks in the second test of 1985. I felt as a boy in the company of men that I had achieved something when I drop-kicked a goal to match his in the first test of that tour.

Ollie Campbell, the Irish grand-master, has a special place in my regard for opposing first five-eighths. Playing against him for Auckland when he was here with the Lions in 1983 was practical education for me. He was difficult to read because of his lightning

Ollie Campbell – the thinking man's fly-half.

ability to think on his feet, to turn an opposition attack into scrambling defence. Every time he took a firm hand in the Lions' fortunes he had us regrouping in some sort of desperation.

It is not surprising that more than a decade after touring here Naas Botha is still South Africa's top fly-half – and even after his lumpy journey of discovery into American football. Naas dictates terms in areas other than his commanding role on the field for Northern Transvaal. He is South Africa's golden boy in every sense of the word. He commands the stage in the overt pay-for-play pantomimes the South African provinces indulge in. He is a player who has founded his record on his prodigious kicking game, so much so that while he was the apple of every Northern Transvaal eye the rest of South Africa lamented the prospective death of rugby through the Northern Transvaal logic that if you have a kicker like Naas, the rest doesn't matter. That is a pity because he was better than that. He could run with a deceptive turn of speed. There was a big power generator in there somewhere and when he went, which was rarely, he could split any defence. He is fiercely competitive, an angry rugby player, an arrogant rugby player and a hell of a good one.

A Rob Andrew is vital to England's plan. In the no-frills, keep-it-ahead-of-the-forwards, tight-minded game England has been committed to, Andrew is the perfect pivot. He copes with pressure better than most, he's gutsy as they come and he has acute perception of the opposition deployment. He is the perfect five-eighths for the dominating forward pack. Scotland's Craig Chalmers, on the other hand, does not have the luxury of an England pack in front of him. He is a cultured player, a busy player, likely to have a defence on through sheer cheek.

Someone who was never going to have anyone on under the old French regime was Didier Camberabero. When the French dedicated themselves to being New Zealanders they saw Camberabero as being their man in that he could more easily be tied down to what they misread as the rigidity of the New

Left: Naas Botha, South Africa's golden boy in every sense of the word. Right: England's Rob Andrew, perfect for the dominating pack.

Didier Camberabero scores one of his three tries against Zimbabwe in the 1987 World Cup. He is better than the player Fouroux made him.

Franck Mesnel – the free spirit of French rugby.

Zealand game. Where a Mesnel could never be hog-tied to that
particular stake, Camberabero could. Mesnel, the free-spirit who
exemplified the most devastating break-back quality of French
rugby, then could not by right command a regular place in the
French line. C'est. incroyable! Camberabero had flair, too, but
was forced to play like a man who feared his wig would fall off.
But his greatest failing was his lack of confidence and probably
that resulted from Fouroux's suffocation of what came naturally.

To fantasise: If I were asked to nominate the overseas player
to take my place in the All Blacks for a crucial game I would,
without hesitation, go for Michael Lynagh. For a start, he speaks
English – or Australian, which is quite close to it – and he may
well have played against New Zealand more than any other
player, so we have familiarity. Michael and I have become
familiar foes. We read each other's play. It's a second-guessing
game. I am conscious always of the quality of his tactical kicking.
In defence I am concerned to cover the ground as fast as I can to
close down his time. If I detect by a gesture, by a hint of body-
language, by a slight shift of stance what Michael is going to do

Michael Lynagh – apologies all round. Should we be playing croquet?

I warn the team. It may be that long, raking kick back to his left, diagonally toward our right wing or full-back, aimed to split the space between them. It may be the dab toward the blind and the chip he does so well.

The Australian forwards of 1990-91 were the best of their country I have seen. This has taken pressure off the inside backs and Michael, in tandem with a superb half-back in Nick Farr-Jones, has become a dominating figure.

It is not my job to cancel out Michael Lynagh, nor his to cancel out me. Lynagh v Fox is the language of the critics. We have had judgment of our respective playing performances based on who kicks more goals. The battle is in other factors. It is the forwards' job to place Michael under pressure by unsettling his forwards and thus unsettling Farr-Jones and the chain reaction goes right through the line. The same applies in reverse to placing pressure on me.

One of the qualities I most admire in Lynagh is that he has not changed as a person from the young guy I first met in 1982. In the rugby environment I would say we were friends. We have never chipped at each other as opponents, neither is hellbent on physical domination of the other. I'd have lost that one, anyway. In a test at Christchurch I accidentally stood on his hand. I apologised. In the heat of the battle I apologised! Had Richard Loe or Sean Fitz heard me I would have been sent to Coventry as some sort of wimp-freak. In an Auckland-Queensland match at Eden Park I went for a close move we call the inside drifter. I get scrum-ball from the half-back, I hold and run at my opposition; the second five-eighths splits wide and runs on an angle toward midfield; the centre comes from behind the second five-eighths and takes the ball from me. It's a target move so the forwards can get to the second-phase set-up and if you think it sounds altogether too complicated for a simple game like rugby I don't know that I blame you. Call it a players' indulgence. On this occasion I let the ball on to Craig Innes as Michael barrelled me in the chest. I grunted and a Fox grunt is not to be dismissed lightly. I thought it was a fair tackle. He thought it was marginally late. He apologised. Dear Diary, should we be playing croquet?

Were I looking for the ideal first five-eighths I would be looking for one with Michael Lynagh's right foot, Nicky Allen's left foot, Ollie Campbell's football brain, Hugo Porta's cheekiness, David Campese's side-step, Michael Jones's instincts, Grant Fox's hands (in all modesty), Carl Lewis's speed, Elton John's rhythm and, considering the daunting size of loose forwards these days, I would build them all into Arnold Schwarzenegger's body. Come to think of it, why limit it to first five-eighths? Give me 15 of those and I'll give you a perfect rugby team.

13

Connubial bliss

This book might never get past the indecency tribunal if I speak too warmly about connubial relationships between consenting adult males in a public place, to wit the middle of a rugby field. It seems that to succeed these days books have to embrace a required element of scandalous behaviour, in about the ratio of one naughty per chapter. I refuse to go that far but the fact is that every time they watch a rugby match the audience is seeing within it two relationships which, if they are not close to connubial bliss, can kill a match stone dead for everyone else on the paddock and the spectators as well.

I refer, of course, to the marriage of the half-backs and the first five-eighths. Like most marriages they can be hell at times but also like most marital relationships practice makes perfect and eventually the good times make up for all else.

In other, less enlightened countries, the half-back and first five-eighths are known by other names – scrum-half and fly-half, scrum-half and stand-off half – but the odd fact is they are required to perform the same functions and maybe nowhere else on the rugby field is a smooth relationship so vital to team performance.

Primarily, the first five-eighths is asking his half-back to deliver a long, fast pass and preferably the ball will be sitting up vertically as it reaches him so he can play with it on his fingertips. If it reaches him lying flat he has to cradle it, pull it into his chest and readjust it as he is deciding just what the devil he is going to do next.

Were it not for Tim Burcher I doubt that I would have become an Auckland player let alone an All Black. I can go on for ever about the hard work I put in, the graft, the sweat and a not inconsiderable amount of blood but had it not been for Tim Burcher's pass I would probably be a winter couch-potato now, starting rumours about All Black conspiracies. Tim was my halfback when I went into the Auckland University team and many times in the Auckland representative team. It was no coincidence that he was the Auckland half-back in 1984 when the backline started to hum and John Hart started to smile. He gave me the room to make me look better than I was. He was not the greatest kicker among half-backs and the way the game is played a half-back needs to be very skilful on the right foot. His logic on kicking was devastatingly simple: "Look, mate, if I can get the ball out there and give you the time you can do it." And the indisputable element was that he could do just that. He could be an effective blindside runner, too, but rarely put his range of skills on display, being content to give the backline the start it needed to run hot. It was a good old-fashioned philosophy and as the beginning of backline success it is as relevant today as ever it was.

Bruce Deans made the pass sit up superbly, too. He was not as long a passer as Burcher but that was secondary to the erect ball-position when it reached me and he was quick to get it airborne, accurate. The first time I really got to know Bruce we were rooming together at the spiritual home of the All Blacks in Auckland, the Poenamo Motor Inn, where more lies are told after matches than in a million election manifestos and where Schwassy, the host, knows more about the politics and intrigues of rugby than the rugby politicians themselves. I walked into our room this day and Bruce was standing on his head. What sort of ding-bat have I got here, I thought. In that pose he was one of the few rugby players I could look down at to talk to. Gidday, I said. Yair, gidday, he said from down there, when's lunch? When's lunch? That was to become familiar. Or when's breakfast or when's dinner? This guy was the ultimate trencherman. He ate a massive cooked breakfast before training, a lunch to satisfy a herd of wayside billy-goats and a dinner to choke a rhino. But he never put on weight. Instead of putting on weight he stood on his head. And he always carried this bag of herbs, probably just something to settle his stomach before the next meal.

Bruce had the highest work-rate of any half-back I played with and a heart like a bull. We were very direct with each other. Like, *very* direct. We both had strong views on the things which would make the combination work effectively, we could debate them with some force but neither of us ever spat the dummy or sulked. We put in the extra hours which can put a gloss on a combination – after-training hours, working at passing and kicking. We were both highly competitive and we competed in

Tim Burcher – without him I may never have played for Auckland.

our practice routines. In that sense we pushed each other, drew new efficiency from each other. He was a physically strong man, undeterred by confrontation with props with blood in their eyes. He could mix it on a par with the big boys almost with an air of gratitude for the relaxation.

We played ten tests together and won ten. Perhaps that statistic as much as the relationship I have discussed might cause the sort of people who deal in unfounded gossip to hesitate before doggedly hammering further capital out of the proposition that there was bitter enmity between Bruce and me and that our relationship on and off the field was verbally and physically abrasive.

Graeme Bachop was one of those All Blacks who suffered most at the whim of the British media at the beginning of the World Cup campaign last year. He was judged to be second-rate and of no threat which, coming from those who most closely follow the fortunes of the Five Nations with their average journeyman scrum-halves, was one of the more pompous judgements of the tournament. Kicking well is the first priority of Five Nations halves where ours is passing. By the end of the tournament there was an unseemly banquet of word-eating and Graeme was dessert of the month.

When he came into the test team on the tour of Wales and Ireland in 1989 he lacked the confidence of one like, say, Deans as a new All Black. A different character altogether from Bruce and with a shy diffidence which probably made my voluble presence over-bearing to him. In natural skill he was a beautiful rugby player even then but just searching for consistency. It was a tribute to the selectors that they perceived what Graeme would become and gave him the time to blossom. It was as if in those early days he tethered his flair and he may well have felt I was an obstacle in the way of loosening it. I would say I did not readily enough adjust to Graeme's inexperience after my give-and-take relationship with Deans. Rather than playing to his instincts with the ball in hand he deferred to me. The result was that he felt inhibited, hesitant.

Finally, he spoke to Grizz about this need he had to be given his head, to cut loose with his own decision-making from time to time. I did not resent that approach though I wished he had had the confidence to talk about it with me. My fault was that while not discouraging, nor did I sufficiently encourage. He felt he knew Grizz better than he knew me and that he needed that starting point. The outcome was startling. Given the license to do his stuff he came strongly into his game. His development on the tour of France in 1990 culminated in two fine tests – quite superb at Nantes. He became much more his own player. After the

Graeme Bachop – dessert of the month.

Nantes test I could tell from his demeanour that his rediscovery of that verve had given him also leaping new confidence in himself. He started poking a little pleasant shit. Now it wasn't always one-way traffic. We were bouncing off each other and it was great for us both.

Now he brings to his game a wonderful range of skills, a positive runner, a fine timer of the pass after making the break and with an amazing ability to pass from anywhere with that whippy, wristy action. He has been criticised for being slow to get the ball on its way but in this he is deceptive because he is able to pass the ball from what ever altitude he receives it. If it is delivered from the lineout at shoulder height he passes it effectively from shoulder-height where others would bring it down into an orthodox passing position.

Mark Adam – a prodigious passer.

I played little rugby with Dave Loveridge but what a class act he was, a world great of the century. I was fortunate in Auckland to have top players like David Kirk, Richard Dunn and a prodigious passer in Mark Adam. And there was Andrew (Shuffles) Donald, a distinctively New Zealand breed of half-back, a farmer, strong, imperturbable and holding a full hand of the specialist disciplines.

They were good years with Kirk for Auckland and New Zealand. We reached the stage where we responded to each other instinctively, a familiarity which bought us time and space. He was not the greatest passer, not the longest, but he was consistently on the spot and a brilliant option-taker. His acute feeling for the blindside break was never better illustrated than in the 1987 World Cup final when, following a French kick-off and the maul, he drifted around the blind, wrong-footed a French drifter or two with a fractional hesitation before bolting 40 metres to set up the second phase and an ebullient try for JK in the corner.

My marriages with half-backs have been the corner-stone of my career. For their quality and their tolerance I thank them – and I owe them.

14

The fab fifteen

I don't know about being a rugby selector. Especially in New
Zealand where nearly everyone is an expert. You could walk
into the bar at the Poenamo the night a touring team is to be
announced and you would find more rugby experts than there
are economic forecasters in New Zealand television land. We're
a nation of experts. Everyone is an expert at something and some
are experts at everything but nowhere are there more experts
than in rugby, unless it is in hammering nails straight, which
happens to be our pioneering heritage.

The strange thing about rugby experts, as with economic
forecasters, is that they cannot agree on anything and when rugby
experts don't agree you have the makings of a marvellous stoush
because rugby in the bar at the Poe – and just about every other
bar in the country – is the most serious matter in the world at any
given time. More serious by far than sex and even slightly more
serious than who piked on shouting their round.

Real selectors are a breed apart. They set themselves up to be
knocked down, jumped on, laughed at, abused, lampooned and
generally punched, bored and screwed by a nation of people who
all know better because they once played left wing for the
Paremata-Plimmerton fourths, coached the Ngakawau fifths or
once watched a video called Rugger Made Easy. God forbid that
I should set myself up as a rugby expert. There's far too much
about the game I don't know. For a start there are too many laws
for what everyone keeps telling us is a simple game. And how,
as a bandy first five-eighths, can I be an expert on the diverse and
devious arts of loosehead propping? What goes on in that dank,
sweaty jungle is a mystery to me. And as for the intricacies of the
power-scrummaging crutch-grip, only the locks and their inti-

Phil Kearns – I want to go to his barby.

mate bedfellows in crutch-gripping, the props, know what that does to a chap's manhood.

And that is why when I set out for your critical appraisal a rugby team comprising the best international players I have played against I do not expect all the experts out there to agree with me. Nor do I expect them to agree among themselves for that is the way of expertise in all things.

In a couple of positions I have drawn on the experience of my two learned friends Mr Steve McDowell QC and Mr Richard Loe LlB, though I doubt their strict impartiality, for props are never beaten by anyone, they are merely given "a bit of a hard time for a while".

Because the performance of a rugby team rises or falls on the work-rate of the tight five it makes sense for all us selectors to sort out our front row and locks first. The hooker will be either Tommy Lawton or Phil Kearns, both of whom, regrettably, are Australians but who, for all that major disadvantage, stand out. Lawton would be the biggest hooker ever to trample a first five-eighths in international rugby. Massive, and with what has become a prime requirement for a hooker in modern rugby, scrummaging power. But I give it to Kearns who, while more demonstrative than Lawton in issuing invitations to the barbecue, scrummages well and has greater mobility. Sean Fitzpatrick has been a great sheet-anchor in the New Zealand scrum because he has that strength in scrummaging and, of course, he can play (by preference) on the wing which makes him the fastest hooker and the slowest wing in world rugby. Kearns has learned much from Fitzy and now he plays frequently on the wing as well but without quite the same polish. It is likely one day we will see them representing their countries on the wing and that will be the day rugby as a spectacle reaches unprecedented heights. The Aussies call Kearns Lightning because he never strikes in the same place twice. This is an unwarranted slur either on his lineout-throwing ability or his

Diego Cash – an entire front-row.

hooking, because he is, quite seriously, very good at both. When it came to the crunch, though, Kearns in preference to Lawton because I want to go to his barby with Fitzy.

Mr McDowell is a loosehead prop who can play tighthead and Mr Loe a tighthead who can play loosehead. This makes them, with Fitzy, who plays hooker or wing, among the most versatile rugby players in the world. As a loosehead, Stevie scrums against tightheads. Because he was reluctant to concede any of his opponents was really up to par he suggested that to save time we name Diego Cash of Argentina tighthead prop, hooker and loosehead prop because he has played in all three positions in test rugby. After a great deal of agony he put in Jean-Pierre Garuet, the uncompromising, grinding Frenchman, and conceded that, along with Cash, Garuet was "Yeah, quite hard for a while, eh". He would not consider Ewen McKenzie on the grounds that there was already an Aussie in the front row.

Richard Loe started to say, "Tony Daly", caught himself and asked who the hooker was. Kearns? That's one Aussie already. I could not argue with his mathematics. Hard luck, Tony, he said, and went straight for Cash who, he said, he really rated. Cash should consider that a monumental accolade.

Dooley, Ackford, Eales, Cutler, McCall, Campbell, Gray, Lorieux. You could mix and match any of them and lock a great scrum. But because there is more to it than locking a scrum I would have Alain Lorieux, on the basis of his greatness in the 1987 World Cup, and Steve Cutler who, even though adding another Australian ingredient, was so dominant in the middle of the lineout. They say locks do not mature until they are 30. If that is so, that other Aussie John Eales will become inter-galactic champion.

Lorieux in the front, Cutler in the middle.

Wade Dooley and Paul Ackford are a great pair for England's

Above: Steve Cutler, to command the middle of the lineout. Left: Alain Lorieux, a champion in 1987.

style but, to my mind, not there when the game really moves.

Assuming this team is going to play the All Blacks I would want Peter FitzSimons as a third lock, even just to come on for the last couple of minutes. Peter would feel deprived if in this company he could not lay down his body at the bottom of a ruck as a willing sacrifice to the New Zealand forwards. He is the most eager pain-victim in the South Pacific outside a Karangahape Road sado-masochism parlour.

Pete gets his orgasms from being autographed by All Black studs (in a manner of speaking). He has written, "In the next ruck I received some unsolicited souvenir autographs from the entire All Black pack that I was able to admire for weeks. Even now, when the morning sun is just right, I am still able to admire the remnants of a few of my more treasured autographs right there in the small of my back." That's why you're the third lock, Pete, because you're a happy victim and when you're happy, we're happy.

Flankers are a problem. Angry, fast flankers are, more specifically, a problem for me. I want a flyer on the open side, but a furious, red-eyed flyer. A Jeff Miller with horns, cloven feet and a lashing tail. I would also like someone else playing first five-eighths for the All Blacks. A great loosie, Jeff, and if I were picking players on admiration I'd go for him or for Simon Poidevin. Both Aussies, of course. Sorry chaps. On the blood-in-the-eye scale I would have to go for Pablo Garreton of the Tucuman Tennis Club, Argentina. He's such a bloody nuisance. He has a genius for playing offside without penalty and any self-respecting footy team has to have one of those. And he'd be good for a game of tennis on Sunday morning.

Then there are the blindsiders, who can do just about everything. Marc Cecillon? John Jeffrey? Willie Ofahengaue? I regret I did not play against Mike Teague at his peak. Because I judge Willie O to be a New Zealander by preference and an Australian by circumstance I doubt that he fits the credentials. Otherwise, on the measure of his awesome rugby in the World Cup '91 he would be it. As it is, I want Poidevin in my pack because he is the ultimate in commitment and courage. And he offers encouragement to those of us who have been around for a while that though you may have retired seven times you can make seven comebacks without recrimination.

The easiest forward to pick in this pack should be the No 8. However, you will understand it causes me great pain. Already there are three Australians in the pack. Messrs McDowell and Loe will have my guts for garters. Without anaesthetic. If this guy were not such a stand-out I would go for someone like France's Laurent Rodriguez playing at his crushing best, or Derek White,

of Scotland...maybe Glenn Ennis, of Canada, or England's Dean
Richards at his bare-legged bloodiest. But none can compare
with Tim Gavin, whose forced absence from the Australian
World Cup team I thought would be a blow from which they
would not recover. He does everything so well, a bonus lineout
jumper deep, a telling force going blind with Nick Farr-Jones
and with a work-rate in the tight beyond most number eights.

Now we may move into the intelligentsia of the game, the
seven players who allow the eight forwards to play their brutal
foot-in-mouth war-games so they may win the ball. I give you the
backs.

I give them to you because whichever way I look at it,
writhing with reluctance, I am top-heavy with trans-Tasman
bottlers. The half-back, as you will have surmised, is Nick Farr-
Jones whose name belongs in the House of Lords but whose heart
is rock-solid colonial. I have cast about among the minnows and
found no-one to come within dwarf-throwing distance of Nick
who is all things to his first five-eighths and all things to his
forwards. He will, of course, captain the team.

Outside Nick there is a little more of a contest, but not one

Nick Farr-Jones, everything a half-back and captain should be.

which would unduly worry Michael Lynagh, he of the tactical kick, the quick pass, the urgent support. He also has the advantage of being a thorough-going gent and a goal-kicker which, you may agree, is a combination of qualities all first five-eighths, including those close to home, do not share. My other contestant is Rob Andrew who, I believe, can play any sort of game England may require of him. But, for the record, Lynagh in a canter.

Let me say this quickly. Tim Horan. Australian. Young. Strong. Great. Attacker. Defender. By a country mile.

Let me say this at greater length. We are now picking our centre. I am looking at Jason Little. He is an Australian. I am also looking at Philippe Sella. He is a Frenchman. Little is the custom-built partner for Horan. Of course he is. Sella is a Rolls Royce rugby player who has suffered from the mad roundabout of French policies yet who, beyond any other, has midfield magic at his fingertips. Which then? Neither. It would be quite outside the bounds of decent civilised behaviour to send a World XV on to the paddock without a representative from the Four Home Countries and, thank heavens, I can justify it on the grounds of quality rather than morality. Because Jeremy Guscott is a quality product with the silken speed, the skills, the step to slot into this team and play like a dream. Before the World Cup I thought his defence was suspect. But there, he was a super tackler.

Other than our own robust lot, wings are the divas of the rugby opera, flighty, quicksilver glory-seekers with clean shorts, clean noses and delicate hamstrings. They are the finishers. Sometimes some of them can be the starters, too. Now take David Campese. Please take him. Anywhere. I have said far too much about him in this book already. He is my right wing. The mother (given the gender anomaly) of all opposition wings. And to cut loose on the left who better than Patrice Lagisquet, that most beautiful player but another pawn in the bizarre game of selection-chess the French have played in recent years. Rory Underwood, a cracker of a try-scorer, Marcello Cuttitti, of Italy, Yoshihito Yoshida, Japan, an explosive little winger, and Jean-Baptiste Lafond (for what he did to that mercurial winger Fitzpatrick) are up there pushing. Picture Lafond. He gets the ball on the blind. He has only three metres to work in and the formidable Fitzy to beat. A bit of a shift, a sway of the hips, a swerve and a jink and Fitzy is staring incredulously at his empty hands. I am rarely guilty even of smiling on the rugby field. On this comic occasion I laughed. For that alone Jean-Baptiste as near as dammit got into my team.

And at fullback, Serge Blanco. Serge the incomparable. For all his temperamental hocus-pocus, no contest. He is one of the magic ones. For this I apologise to my old buddy Gavin Hastings

Serge Blanco – one of the magic ones; no contest.

who, were he not opposed by someone from wonderland, would be in my team.

So there you have it:

Diego Cash   Phil Kearns   Jean-Pierre Garuet

Alain Lorieux   Steve Cutler

Pablo Garreton   Simon Poidevin

Tim Gavin

Nick Farr-Jones

Michael Lynagh   Tim Horan

Jeremy Guscott

Patrice Lagisquet   David Campese

Serge Blanco

I leave it to the experts to chew-up, spit-out and grind into the dust. Believe me, I understand. No hard feelings, honest. I willingly defer to better judgement. Honest I do.

15

On being Auckland

If statistics are the trivia of rugby they can also be the arch liars, the cold facade hiding the drama, the sweat and the tears of matches won and lost. They will not, for instance, show that the Auckland Ranfurly Shield era was built on a resounding loss to Canterbury two seasons before the era started and on a disputed result against Counties in its second defence.

The Canterbury match was the Ranfurly Shield challenge of 1983, the season after John Hart in his first year as coach had taken an untried Auckland team through to the National Championship. Auckland went to Canterbury and lost 31-9 to a Grizz Wyllie-trained team whose commitment and fitness playing to a plan were a revelation. Canterbury were fitter than Auckland in the 80-minute grind of a hard match and at the end of it my impression as a young player trying to find his feet was that had the game gone 160 minutes that ruthless Canterbury machine would still have been running at me. They set out by plan to snuff out the threat Andy Haden was to them in the lineout, achieved that and with efficiency and at speed took Auckland apart.

The process of annihilation was something every Canterbury player wanted to be part of. Every player was fit enough to be part of it until the end. They knew they would win and they knew how they would win. For all the qualities Canterbury had that day fitness was the single factor without which the grand plan could have disintegrated. And it was that message which burned in John Hart's mind even as he acknowledged Canterbury's great performance.

It was, of course, the Jim Blair factor. And it was upon the Jim Blair factor that Hart then set out to give substance to the dream he had for Auckland rugby. Aucklanders who take pride in the

The Jim Blair factor gave substance to John Hart's dream. Here, at right, he works with a more recent half-back, Jason Hewett.

achievements of the provincial team through the years following the lifting of the Shield in 1985 should paste in their hats, "Saturday, September 24, 1983, Lancaster Park, Canterbury 31, Auckland 9," for that was the most significant date of the decade for Auckland, more significant even than that of the successful challenge of 1985, for without it there may not have been a successful challenge.

Following the lifting of the Shield in 1985 we had two defences. We won the first against Waikato well, really well. And then we beat Counties 12-9 in a game Richard Fry, the Counties five-eighths, detected he could dominate with some towering bombs. At the end of it Counties, who had been magnificently led by Andy Dalton, looked back on a refereeing decision which they were adamant had cost them a try and the Ranfurly Shield. Their No 8, Dave Trombik, certainly crashed over the line after another Fry up-and-under but the referee smiled upon Auckland and awarded a five-metre scrum from which we escaped. From the utter euphoria of the Shield match against Canterbury, through

Auckland, having won the Ranfurly Shield in the great game of 1985 at Lancaster Park, is about to come back to earth. Counties, under Andy Dalton, did just about everything but get the referee's nod.

the comprehensive Hart-dream victory over Waikato and then to the heavy dumpling-in-the-guts performance against Counties there were experiences Hart was delighted his team should have had at that time. It meant that instead of going off into the summer with something like smug indifference to the requirements for the next winter his team was back to earth. Counties had shown that in Ranfurly Shield rugby taking things for granted spelled danger and possibly disaster.

As the era developed, Auckland's approach and that of the All Blacks had distinct parallels. The Ranfurly Shield holder is always going to get players in the All Blacks and Auckland was playing a style of game the players enjoyed and the public wanted to see. It was a difficult style to combat with a great tight

The John Hart half-time style. . .no-one in the team by right.

five giving loosies and backline the start they needed. Hart had
worked out the game he wanted to play and picked the players
to do it – just as the All Black selectors did in 1987.

I have said that my part in the realisation of the Hart vision
was a stuttering thing in the early years, when I needed reassurance
of my right to be there. In 1984 when things were really rolling
in his 15-man game an ingredient which I had never really
experienced in rugby added another dimension to my love of the
game. It was fun. I had always enjoyed my rugby but it was an
enjoyment based on such serious matters as doing things right,
on what I could achieve and had achieved in efficiency through
working at it. It was an enjoyment which came from my years of
translating that efficiency into winning. But fun? Never. In those
years Auckland gave me the fun that comes with being part of an
exhilarating expression of rugby.

Hart never allowed any player, no matter who – a Haden, a
Whetton, a Stanley, a McDowell, a Drake – the luxury of believing
he was in the team by right. It did not generate a fear which made
you apprehensive. It was more a suspicion of your vulnerability
which sharpened the instinct for the game and the desire to be
part of this team. From the players' perspective the Auckland
carnival started in 1984.

There is a perception that Auckland is strong because it has to be strong with its vast call on players. But from 1976 through 1981 Auckland, with that vast resource, won nothing. Harnessing the talent and making representative rugby an exciting goal were Hart's achievements. He talent-spotted and he kept injecting fresh vitality into the squad. He had Sean Fitzpatrick to step in for Iain Abercrombie, Bernie McCahill for Kurt Sherlock. He scandalised sceptics by bringing in the raw kid Kirwan from third grade. He converted Lindsay Harris from five-eighths to the dashing fullback he became. He took a 20-year-old loose forward named Jones from the Waitemata club and set him on the way to becoming a world star. It was a programme which found 14 Auckland players representing New Zealand in the World Cup of 1987, six backs – David Kirk, Bernie McCahill, Joe Stanley, John Kirwan, Terry Wright and myself – and eight forwards – John Drake, Sean Fitzpatrick, Steve McDowell, Gary Whetton, Alan Whetton, Michael Jones, Mark Brooke-Cowden, Zinzan Brooke.

As individuals and as a team we were set standards to play to. We felt that if we played to those standards week by week opposition teams would find us a difficult team to beat. Some sides could stay with us for 60 minutes then, just as with the All Blacks, we went away from our opposition in the last 20.

The range of the Auckland game meant the wings were scoring tries and that Harris was scoring tries from fullback. It was, in a sense, a mirror-image of the way All Black rugby would go.

When Maurice Trapp took over in 1987 he, with his assistant, Bryan Williams, recognised their inherited players were part of a special team with a winning formula. Where Hart solicited player-input off the training field, they encouraged it as an active training policy. Maurice was the quiet regulator, never domineering but nor was he to be domineered. As young players came in they would certainly detect a strong senior-player influence but always in collaboration with the Trapp-Williams combo whose philosophy it was to call in that influence. And it was part of their strength that, while being able to use their players in this way, they ran the ship. When they retired after the 1991 season Auckland had maintained the winning habit.

They had also kept in place a strong development programme which enabled them to feed in players like Craig Innes, Eroni Clarke, Olo Brown, Robin Brooke, Shane Howarth, Brett Iti, Va'aiga Tuigamala, Mark Carter. I had new half-back partners like Jason Hewett, who came to Auckland from Manawatu and immediately showed why he was an international prospect, and occasionally Ant Strachan, a former Otago player, a beautiful clearer of the ball and, in an almost self-effacing way, a real work-machine, efficient, rarely in serious error.

Of all the selections for the "new" All Blacks to play the centennial matches against the World XV this year Strachan's was the one which took most New Zealanders off guard, perhaps not so much after the final trial but that he was at the trials at all...that the selectors had the astuteness to see that in this representative part-timer there was the sort of half-back to be an integral part of their reforms. And here, too, was a beginning for Eroni Clarke, a midfielder who, like Innes, had been brought into the highly-pressured rugby of the national championship as a wing.

It is a risky business to be seen in some way to be defending Auckland these days. There has been, in varying degrees of intensity, a complex out there about Auckland and Auckland rugby. I think it has something to do with success, something to do with, I suppose, the boredom of having the Ranfurly Shield rest with one holder for so long, something to do with the big city thing. It is unmistakably there, yet any reaction from Auckland to it is now seen to be caused by some sort of persecution complex.

The players are merely players. They are as strongly dedicated to doing well for their teams as, say, Steve Hotton is for Otago, Laurence Hullena for Wellington, Andrew McCormick for Canterbury, Phil Coffin for King Country, Marty Berry for Wairarapa-Bush...we're a small country and Auckland rugby players feel no special status in it other than the pride they have in playing for Auckland. The fact is that the Ranfurly shield probably means less to Auckland as a city than it has to Canterbury, to Hawke's Bay, to Taranaki and to others in the past like Waikato and Otago.

Auckland's very size and cosmopolitan spread of population dictates that the fever which hit such close-knit communities as Hawke's Bay and Taranaki and Waikato and, to a large extent, Canterbury is not for us. Auckland supporters are a wonderful part of rugby but I doubt that there is the same generation of warmth as in other places and certainly not the same intensity and possessiveness about the Shield.

When we have taken the Shield away we have been criticised for not taking it to major unions. The idea of taking the trophy to smaller unions was that it was there that such matches would bring the greatest benefit. Had all of New Zealand been able to feel the atmosphere in a place like Te Kuiti, to become saturated in its joy and its rain, to see how rugby scored, there could have been no criticism that we took it there rather than to, say, Wellington or Dunedin. The people of the King Country came to see their boys take on the city slickers and do well. But they also

Ant Strachan, the part-timer who became a New Zealand trials sensation and an All Black.

Eroni Clarke eased through first-class rugby on the wing and swept into the All Blacks at second five-eighths.

wanted to see Auckland performing at peak. On a rough day it was one of my most uplifting rugby experiences anywhere. Playing in Nelson was much the same.

It is not the fault of the players that what others see as "the Auckland media machine" creates stars out of young players before their time but it certainly rebounds on the players. There would be more point in the supporters of some other unions feeling aggrieved about more important matters: that in challenging Auckland for the Ranfurly Shield their teams have had a defensive phobia – "We can't win the game but we'll keep the bloody score down." And that is not the way to win the Shield.

In its matches against Auckland, Hawke's Bay epitomises to me what challengers should be striving for. Simply, points. Simply, to raise the spirit for the occasion and turn it into attacking rugby, using whatever ball becomes available to have a crack at the defenders. The team which has the attacking spirit will be the one to beat Auckland. I doubt that the one which goes out to stop us will. The acclaim is better deserved by those who take it to us to score points while losing than those whose planned strategy for the day is to keep the Auckland scoring down.

16

Kicking for kicks

If you have the chance to watch Don Clarke kicking the goal for which he is most renowned, that extraordinary demonstration of concentration and judgement across the Athletic Park storm against the French of 1961, you will note that from the time he makes the final adjustment to the ball his eyes drill into one spot on it, never wavering, the head still as a rock as he retreats from it, then a sighter through the seam as he settles at the end of the run and again the intense focus on the point of impact until the strike is made.

If you read *Bob Scott on Rugby*, his book with TP McLean, you will find: "Now pace slowly backward, keeping steady and keeping your eye on the point of the ball that you intend to kick. Pay no attention to anything but the ball...You are serene, nothing is disturbing you, the crowd is the noise of the surf on the beach, your team-mates, your opponents, all are thousands of miles away, there is nothing in eternity but you and the rugby ball..." And Scott stresses the need for hard work if there is to be reward from kicking.

The more things change the more they are the same. Scott in the '40s and '50s, Clarke in the '50s and '60s were two of the greatest of goal-kickers when "around the corner" was no more than a helpful tip to a lost traveller. They were toe-kickers from a straight run. Now toe-kickers are almost as rare as three-point tries but while the mathematics have changed the essentials remain.

Talking about kicking is first talking about the tools. In this I speak for myself because there is no one pair of boots to suit everyone. When I play for Auckland I wear Adidas because they best suit me. When I play for New Zealand I wear Mizuno, the

New Zealand Rugby Union sponsor's product, and although my test average is minimally higher than my Auckland average I do have a preference for Adidas. Whichever boot I wear, however, my requirements are the same. I look for boots which are hardly there. Boots which most closely approximate bare feet. The lightest of the light. Simple boots. No wedges to raise the heel, no extra bits of coloured leather for adornment. None of what Brian Lochore would call "Flash Harry" bits. The leather must be soft and supple, the sole flexible but stable – the key to the boot. And if you were to say I was very bloody particular, pernickety even, I would agree with you.

The ball. Now there's a vexatious subject. But it doesn't matter how vexatious it is. You play with what you are given and you get yourself used to it very, very quickly. The penalty for not getting used to it is death. I am not a fan of synthetic balls but I accept the ridiculously-obvious reality that a white synthetic is more visible to television viewers than a brown leather and while they have not yet been able to recreate the wonderfully secure feeling of leather they are working at it. What's more, in difficult conditions the synthetic can be less treacherous than the leather.

Much was made of the difficulties kickers had with the synthetic World Cup ball. My only criticism of it was that it was too light and then it was up to me to modify my technique to get it right. The fact is that Adidas was asked to produce a ball weighing 430 grammes. The maximum allowable in law is 440 grammes. The Adidas Universal leather we use here is 450 grammes – a little overweight but a cracker to kick. All kickers know the heavier ball is better but the brain-surgeons asked the manufacturer to produce World Cup balls at 430 grammes, 10 grammes lighter than the maximum. Does that not seem distinctly contrary? My understanding is that the manufacturers carried the can while the decision-makers covered up. It is said we are allowed 9-10lbs of pressure but a ball functions much better at 12. I would be surprised if other kickers did not feel much the same. The bare bones of it, however, are that a good tradesman will make the adjustment. I only know that when I am kicking goals in Paradise or Purgatory I want a 450 gramme leather with 12lbs of pressure.

There are matters of technique which are not to be tampered with. However, in the build-up to the placement of the ball you may express your own fancy for sand, sawdust, a tee or you may damage your heel by digging a hole. I like sand and I hate tees because they don't give me the flexibility in strong winds or difficult underfoot conditions to vary the height of the ball.

The only no-no placing the ball is that it must not lean

The place. Upright. OK.

Leaning slightly forward. OK. Contact point is the blue point.

Leaning back. No view of contact point. Wrong.

The seam dead verticle. No lean left or right.

Preparation. Left foot width of hips, line of instep points to posts. Right.

Instep pointing left. You will hook. Wrong.

Instep pointing right. You will slice. Wrong.

Ankle in line with sideseam. You will hit ball at bottom of swing. Right.

Ankle behind sideseam. You will hit ball on the up and hook. Wrong.

Ankle too far forward. You will hit ball on downward swing and slice. Wrong.

The action. Eyes down, watching contact point, left shoulder coming forward, weight on ball of foot.

The vital plant of left foot, width from ball ideal, instep pointing straight, eyes on contact point.

Left arm pointing ahead for correct balance. Eyes still down. Kicking contact on bone of instep.

The follow-through, having kicked right through the ball, weight still going forward, kicking foot straight and high. It's a goal.

What it's all about.

backward, not even fractionally. It must lean slightly forward or stand straight up. You should not be concerned merely to kick the ball as an object. Your concern is to hit the contact point on it. If the ball is leaning a little forward you can see the contact point clearly. If it is upright you can see it. If it is leaning backward you cannot see it. It has nothing to do with aerodynamics or academic claptrap like that. It is simply the ease with which you may see the point of contact. I use the seams to get my flight-path, to line up the posts and to make sure the ball is not tilting right or left.

Should you be a left-footer please read what follows in the mirror. If that is indecipherable just take the points, convert them to your leftness and kick the goals.

How you retreat to the end of your run-up does not matter. There is not a right way or a wrong. I notice Greg Alexander, the Penrith league team kicker, takes his lateral strides first and then moves back to his starting point from there. You should find your own way back to that crucial point which is the beginning of your arced run. Were you to copy me you would attract some vocal discouragement from the crowd but for the record I take six very deliberate, balanced paces back and then two to the left for kicks outside the 22. From the 22 or closer and 15 metres or more in from touch I take four back and two across.

The run-up must create an arc. An instep-kicker should not run straight at the ball because when he gets to the kicking position he will only be swinging his leg rather than using his hip to generate power. He must create the arc. It is crucial.

The most important single factor, providing you have done everything else correctly, is where you place your non-kicking foot. It must be the width of your hips away from the ball. You must have the freedom to open the hip up and shut it. If you place that non-kicking foot too close to the ball you will only push your leg at the ball. Your non-striking ankle should be in line with the cross-seam and your non-striking foot must point at the target – the goalposts.

Having your arc and your foot-placement right brings your shoulder forward so you are not kicking open-chested. The shoulder is up, the head directly above the ball. Otherwise, open-chested, head off-line, you have bought a ticket in a kicking lottery and the odds are longer than a wet summer. Your arms become your balancing pole. To keep your left shoulder up your left arm must be anywhere between 45 degrees and directly ahead. It must not be straight out to the side because that would open up your chest. The right arm tends to follow naturally just down and behind your right hip.

Nothing is new under the sun. When you play a cover-drive at cricket you do not play it open-chested. You play it with the

The more things change the more they are the same. Round-the-corner kicking is yet to come but Don Clarke, above, and Bob Scott, right, create their balance and have their eyes pinned to the point of contact.

head forward over the ball and hit through it. Tennis, golf...

Now if you have done those things it will bring your kicking foot into play to hit the ball precisely at the bottom of its swing, giving you maximum power and control. Golfers use their hips and drive through the ball. The principle is the same. You have struck the point of contact with the instep bone. You should finish up on the toes of your left foot, still balanced, while following through on the kick as high as you can with your right.

Your areas of error are specific. If your left instep points to the left of the posts the ball will go left and if it points to the right the ball will go right – the hook and the slice. If it is behind the ball you will tend to hook and if it is too far in front you will slice. Precision in placement of the left foot is everything. If your left foot is too wide you will be off balance. You will have to lean over and the chances are you will not get a stable plant with that non-kicking foot.

Should you miss the goal it isn't your boot and it isn't the ball. You have done something which, technically, is wrong. Instinctively, you analyse and know why you have missed so you will make the appropriate adjustment next time. When my boot strikes the ball I know whether the goal is there. I don't need to wait and study the flight. I know from the contact and the feel where the ball has gone. If everything is sweet I turn and run back. Some commentators watch the kicker not the posts and call the goal by his demeanour.

Relaxation is the other mental-physical partnership. How you achieve it is up to you. I use a technique called mental rehearsal. I have in my mind a picture of the ball going through the posts. The deep breathing, the shaking of the hands, are to rid the body of tension so that all is crystal-clear and unperturbed in the mind – the picture is in focus. I command myself, "Head down. Follow through."

If the ground is slippery I slow down my run. I estimate the extent to which that will shorten my distance and I compensate. I cannot afford to have the plant-foot slip. If there is wind – and there is 95 per cent of the time – you must try to estimate how far it is likely to push the ball off-course and compensate for it. Had Don Clarke not compensated for the wind that day at Athletic Park his kick would have cleared the fence at the Basin Reserve, three kilometres due north. A kicker's favourite ground is the one he plays on most. Its vagaries are his allies.

For the set-piece drop-kick, whether at the kick-off or the called shot at goal you apply the identical principles as for the place-kick. You drop the ball so it ends up as if you had placed it. The other mechanics apply. The snap-shot at goal under pressure, off-balance? Hope.

The punt will go in the direction of the instep assuming you strike it fairly. The embarrassing screwed punt off the side of the foot should only occur in pressure situations – and that's little excuse. The longer you want to kick the closer to the ground you hit the ball; the higher you want to hoist it, the higher off the ground you hit it. With a spiral punt you cannot by design kick an off-break or a leg-break into touch. The grubber you can control more, but these are kicks of snap-judgement. With the chip you can help by tumbling the ball backward end over end but the pitch and bounce are over to the eccentric shape of a rugby "ball", which in the name of accuracy should have been named something else. A rugby egg. A rugby oval. A bloody nuisance (when it bounces the wrong way). A thing of beauty (when it is in the hand or leaving the boot).

The bounce is one of the delicious eccentricities of rugby. A superbly-judged kick can turn to crap at the moment of contact with the earth. At North Harbour's Onewa Domain in 1991 I received the ball from second-phase on attack. Their backs were flatter than a pint of old English bitter. There was no way we were going to get the ball through the line. But who should I spot lurking out there like a Fitzpatrick-wing but Michael Jones. Leaner than Fitzy, measurably faster than Fitzy but no hungrier for tries than Fitzy. So I slotted one over for him. He collected it and scored. Great kick, Foxy, they said, great kick. I would say it was a convenient tactic of the moment and the kick was well-judged. But the greatness lay with the crazy ball and the manner in which it elected to bounce. And Michael Jones.

I practice kicking as my preparation for the game. Just as in team training we simulate the match situation, so it is with kicking. You do not forget how to do it – just like riding a bike or, less boringly, bonking. And, as in both those pursuits, it helps to have a natural feel for the rhythm of it. Interesting that the old All Black prop Ian Clarke, elder brother of Don, was a kicking natural. There you had a family of footballers out in the farm paddocks kicking the ball around from the time they were kids. When Ian drop-kicked that marvellous 40-metre goal from a mark for the Barbarians against the All Blacks at Cardiff Arms in 1964 it was a result of years of doing what came naturally. Another who has much the same ability is John Drake, our World Cup prop of 1987. He has pulled in plenty of suckers on drop-kick bets – a couple of jugs a kick and he didn't have to buy a beer all winter. A hustler.

So you have, desirably, but not essentially, that bit of natural feel for kicking. After that there are three major requirements: work, work, work. Or, if you like, practice, practice, practice. And it helps no end to be playing for a team to create the pressure to force the opposition into the lapses which give the goal-kicker his opportunity. That has been my huge bonus playing for the All Blacks and for Auckland.

The day before every match, mostly on the match ground, for provincial games as well as test matches and all tour matches, I go through my set routines, kicking from set positions on the field.

I start on the middle of the 22 with three shots, move 10 metres right for three more and then 15 metres from touch, three more. I repeat the exercise on the left side of the field.

I take the ball back 10 metres from the 22 and go through the whole thing again. Then on the 10-metre line I take three shots from the centre, two from the right 15-metre mark and two from the left 15-metre mark. I do not move to a new mark until all the allotted shots from each point are successful.

Sometimes I will go back to the middle of half-way and kick from there. Then I wipe away some sweat, heave a sigh, and go back to the 22-metre line, five metres from the right touch, two shots, and from 15 metres from touch two shots from the shorter run. From the left side of the field I repeat the dose. Then just to the left of the uprights, two shots, and the same from the right.

For 45 minutes, rain, sleet, snow, gales, tropical sun and bloody-minded mixes of all of them, I go out and do it. Forty-nine shots at goal not counting those I may kick from half-way. I have never knocked over all 49 first go. The closest I came to the perfect first-up score was at King's Park, Durban, when I kicked 51 from 52 shots including three from half-way, and the one I missed was the first from the middle of the 22 – and that hit an upright.

After all this I practice a few drop-outs, kick-offs and up-and-unders but at that stage I do not give them much time. In the domestic season I get to training an hour early and do tactical kicking and drop-outs for 30-45 minutes. On tour I do the same after training.

Throughout it all I am thinking the match scene, feeling the match scene. I have that sharp-edged picture in my mind and I have locked out all other considerations. I am not practising for anything other than ensuring I am mentally prepared. Now it does not worry me if I have a rough day at practice because I know it does not portend a rough day in the match. I used to pack deep, deep sads, go into monkish contemplation, when two or three, maybe four, days a year my kicking success ratio was not 50 per cent. Now it's a straw in the wind and my beer is as sweet after those matches as after a 100 per cent gig.

It's not easy to give advice without sounding self-righteous or self-satisfied or just plain pompous, but I will take that risk. If you have the goal-kicking talent don't sit back on your ability.

Don't be like the talented player who thinks it is good enough to be a talented player when with the will and the work he could be a great one.

The work. Aye, there's the rub. Who was it who said that? Shakespeare or Loe?

17

Why bother?

The Auckland-Canterbury no-scrum fiasco when, after the ordering-off of the Canterbury hooker, John Buchan, the match proceeded with tap-kicks instead of scrums should be put down as a one-off divertissement, never to be repeated.

After that match there were those who commended the spectacle as "showing what rugby could be with a little tinkering with the laws". That particular little tinkering with the laws turned a rugby match into some other sort of sport in which, effectively, one of the game's most desirable elements, that which makes it a game for people of all physiques, was erased. Were that to become the new character of rugby we would have to find a new name for it because it wouldn't be the rugby which has become the sport of New Zealanders of all shapes and sizes.

So we have the elimination of the scrum. Goodbye Richard Loe, Steve McDowell, Graham Purvis, Laurence Hullena, Olo Brown and all your rugby progeny. What shall we hit next? The lineout. Let's scrub the lineout. It's just a cesspool of infringements anyway. Who needs it? Goodbye Ian Jones, Blair Larsen, Mark Cooksley, Adrian McKenzie, David Mayhew and all your rugby heirs.

And if we get rid of scrums and lineouts it seems pretty useless persevering with rucks and mauls. They're pretty dull unless you happen to be at the bottom of one. There must be easier, more convenient, less harrowing ways of getting the ball back into motion. Forget their presence as a forward skill and make this a game for backs only. Let's have another tinker with the laws and bar all players who can't run 100 metres in 11.5 seconds. Now we're really getting a game that moves. No scrums, no lineouts, no rucks, no mauls, no power. A game for 30 Terry Wrights.

Rugby. . .a game for 30 Terry Wrights?

Tinkering with the laws has produced what must be a phenomenon in sport: Rugby players at the top level who don't intimately know the laws of the game they represent. Tinkering with the laws has seen the law-makers siring a monster. Rugby, the simple game, has become rugby, the most complicated game in the whole world of sport. And if it is so complicated that its players cannot absorb and understand all its laws then, indeed, something should be done about it. But what is done to it should not make it another game.

I can remember seeing and reading the rules of rugby as they were in the 1890s. The book was little more than a few scraps of paper. Now it is an intimidating tome. Back in the 1950s before I was any sort of consideration to anyone there were only about 30 reasons to penalise. Now there are more than 100. By the year 2020 will there be 200? Referees have told me that, working by the book, they would award a penalty or free kick at every lineout. Some of the technical lineout infringements have now become free-kick offences and that is a blessing of sorts. But lineout technicalities of the most irritating sort remain and bring added delays because they are sternly policed. For instance, the strictly-applied metre gap between the lines of forwards involves delays before the ball is thrown in. By its strict enforcement pedantry is given another boost. In such matters, and others in the lineout, the pedantic referee is given the power to have an undue influence on the game. What has happened in lineout "tinkering" since the days of shoulder-to-shoulder jumping, two-handed taking with blocking and wedging and quick delivery is the most severe indictment of this compulsion to change without thinking ahead to all the consequences.

Should referees, with a sudden rush of blood, decide universally that they will rule by the book in every area of the game rugby would sink like a stone, never to be seen again.

The endeavour in recent times has been to try to keep the ball in play more often, thus increasing the flow of the game and its attractiveness to its audience. Admirable. But the result must be achieved by means which do not smack of turning rugby into 15-man rugby league. The end result of that, of course, would be one game. I say without animosity to league that for this country, at least, that would be a bad thing. Having the two games is a desirable condition in the fabric of our society.

So why have we been looking to change the game? First, I suggest, for the patently wrong reason that we are being reactive to the spectacle of Australian rugby league on television – a brilliantly-packaged and projected image of the sport. Second, there has been growing concern, fed by published statistics, about the amount of time the ball is in play. In their baldness, these can be dramatic, even damning, statistics and especially so when set alongside statistics which show how much longer the ball is in play in rugby league. We have two different games. Rugby union has lineouts, and scrums which really are scrums. Both are essential to the character of the game and to the attractiveness of the game to its players. It has, too, rucks and mauls – that is, mauls which are specific to ball-release to the running backs as opposed to what was becoming an obsession with interminable rolling mauls and long-delayed delivery.

There was that ill-advised effort to de-power the scrum at all levels. As a means of cutting back and, possibly, eliminating neck and back injuries to physically immature players it was a well-taken decision. But at the top level of provincial rugby it was a public relations disaster – and I speak here of the effect it had on players whose major role in the game was in bringing profit to their team through their scrummaging expertise. And expertise is assuredly what it is. The forwards themselves might prefer to have it described as an art form.

New Zealand in 1992 sings the praises of great props and locks from the recesses of its rugby history...the Ken Grays, the Wilson

Outlaw power-scrummaging and the pushover try? Farewell to the front-row club, here represented by Sean Fitzpatrick, Laurence Hullena and Steve McDowell.

Whinerays, the Kevin Skinners, the Johnnny Simpsons and the Tiny Whites, the Bob Duffs the Colin Meadses, the Nev MacEwans. We have a game rich in the tradition of great tight forwards. Why seek to kick that to touch by giving the new generation less and less encouragement to flex their muscles? De-power the scrum, ban the push-over try (as was recommended) and teams might as well play eight Michael Joneses. The reason behind Canterbury's flirtation with the laws in that match against Auckland was that they were getting a dorking in the scrums. They took an opportunity within the laws to negate that superiority. I have no criticism of Canterbury, but of the law-makers I have. It was an example of hurried legislation, not thought through – and that, in these days of frenetic government, has a familiar ring to it.

Rugby union does not need to toy with its character as a game to meet what is a perfectly justifiable call for greater activity. The character of rugby league is its own and, in all that time the ball is in play, it enables players with certain duties to relax and, in effect, take a breather at times. When the ball is in play in rugby union 30 players are on the go. It is a fundamental difference between the codes. Given new laws to ensure the ball is in play as much as in league, rugby union would be staring total professionalism in the face. The players could not remain amateur while turning to the game the full time to achieve such levels of fitness as have not even been thought of thus far.

Of course it is admirable to aim to increase the flow of the game. There are other ways of achieving it than to take rugby into a revolution it does not need. Consider penalties and free kicks. Consider, too, the jungle of the lineout. Referees say they could penalise or allocate free kicks at every lineout but they don't – presumably, for the sake of the game. It seems extraordinary to me that having undertaken not to award penalties or free kicks at every lineout, referees should then take action against players at the front or middle of the lineout for such offences as barging or holding or crossing the line or whatever (short of violently foul play), while the ball is being won cleanly at the back for quick delivery to the backs with the game firing. Or, likewise, whistling back-of-the-lineout shenanigans, while the ball is won and ready for delivery from the middle or front. Those hiccups are at the root of the stop-start rugby which so often comes under criticism and which, under new laws, persist even with the enforced metre gap. Forwards are not going to play new-image rugger rules in the lineout.

I have absolute respect for the people who turn their free time to rugby as referees. I wonder, though, whether clinical appraisal of them by their judgement panel in the grandstand is not a constraining influence. Within the context of their practical examination is the flow of the game sufficiently an element? What influences a referee to take it upon himself to allocate blame for a collapsed scrum when really he does not know why it collapsed?

Collapsing scrums are more a matter of vexation for the players than for the referees. The reason for this is that the cause of a scrum collapse very often is not fairly ruled because the referee is ruling by guess and by God. Such is the club-environment of the front row that God is not admitted so there is little point in the referee calling on Him to verify his own guesswork. Steve McDowell, frustrated with refereeing calls on collapsing, has tested referees out and found that the call is often made with no knowledge at all of where the blame lies. It is not uncommon for a scrum to collapse because one side is unable to bear the legal scrummaging pressure of the other. But penalties result. Referees must know, not guess, before making decisions upon which the result of a game could hang.

The international law-makers have shown clear vision by virtually guaranteeing more running attack by the simple means of allocating the throw-in to the kicking side following a penalty kick to touch. I am surprised the law as it used to be was allowed to exist for so long while so much irrelevant "tinkering" went on. It made no sense. More often than not the kick took the non-offending side into an attacking situation. Then the offending side was given an odds-on chance of getting the ball back from the lineout and booting it back downfield. Stop, start, stop.

By its very size the lawbook encourages stop-start rugby and this encourages spectators to judge the game by the extent of bum-numbness. When a spectator becomes conscious his bum is getting numb he's not watching much of a game. In this age of polls it might be enlightening to institute a numb-bum poll on rugby. It would provide a more legitimate cause for changing laws than changing them in fear of league.

I am glad the new laws outlaw the baulk-pass from the half-back. While that was outside the spirit of the game, not so the dummy-run without the ball. That is a fair tactical ploy provided the No 8 is immediately active within the tactic and not just holding the ball in at the back of the scrum. Should he hold the ball in the back while the half-back dummy-runs that must be a penalty offence under baulking. Opposition "off-side" on the dummy-run side of the field should be ignored if it does not give an unfair advantage.

It was not surprising that matches from the quarter-final at the World Cup came under less pressure from the referees. The rigidity with which, by decree, they had policed the ball-killing by players going over the top threatened the whole tournament with viewing disaster. Here was the diamond-studded opportunity for rugby to express itself to the world as a spectacle and the referees were whistling the game into oblivion. Someone pressed the button at quarter-final time and the robotic whistling of the rucks ceased. It is vital that the deliberate killing of the ball be blown off the park but here the referees were indiscriminate, making no allowance for what clearly were accidental breaches with players being forced over the top by driving forwards coming in behind and sometimes the ball available to the non-offending side anyway.

I take strong issue with the drop-kick from halfway after a converted try or a penalty goal. The drop-kick is an extremely difficult kick, with technique seriously impaired by muddy conditions. This means it can be a problem using it as an attacking weapon from a kick-off. Nor does it make sense to have a drop-kick off after a missed conversion as we have now. It should be a place-kick at all times and if the match officials are on the job there will be sand at the half-way point by the time the kicker gets up there. This would encourage kickers to kick short to create second-phase attack immediately for one team or the other.

Dr Roger Vanderfield, as chairman of the International Rugby Board last year, said the World Cup had changed the game forever. He sure said a mouthful. More than 100 countries took the television coverage of the tournament and the game was discovered, too, by mass circulation newspapers and magazines which previously had given it space measured in peanuts. But he was saying much, much more than that the game was now truly international. He was saying, I hope, that the game must now face up to such complications and responsibilities as through the years it has been desperately trying to sweep under the carpet. It has to cease puking with distaste and speak the unspeakable. "Professionalism" is not so hard to say without gagging.

International rugby is at the cross-roads. Go blindfolded to the left and a continuation of the unfair pressure on players and inevitable strife with the players. Go open-eyed to the right and an understanding of the players' dilemma and urgent action to create an environment through which the players are granted by right the means to give to the game the time its administrators are demanding. Failing that, let them reaffirm the game as a strictly amateur code, cut back the schedule of tours to the bare bones it used to be – no more than five tests a year, three at home and two overseas – get the players back into their clubs and forget the promotion of the game, on the backs of the players, as a vast commercially-opulent enterprise. To my mind that would take more guts than making the move into player payments at a

Dr Roger Vanderfield. . ."The World Cup has changed the game forever."

realistic level and I have no doubt it will not be seen to be an
option.

It is ironic, then, is it not, that few players want to be paid to
play, that few want what would seem on the surface to be the
sublime condition of being paid to play the game they love? I do
not. I do dream of an idealistic sort of "professionalism" with
players contracted to their unions in the promotion of rugby
through merchandising, through the attraction of sponsorships,
through endorsements, through coaching – no prizemoney, no
bonuses, no transfer fees; simply a form of self-funding em-
ployment by the rugby unions.

Should the four Home Unions find a proposition of this sort
beyond the pale then may the New Zealand and Australian

Rugby Unions – I would have no doubt with the aggressive support of the South African Rugby Union – spell out for them the hard facts of life in the colonies and stake out their independence, not as a threat of secession but as a promise to administer their own reforms.

It is interesting that on a visit to New Zealand early in the 1992 winter Australia's Rod McCall said for Wellington's Dominion newspaper, "Unless officials give more thought to the demands they're placing on players, problems are going to occur. I can sympathise to an extent with the state unions and the Australian union. The win in the World Cup has increased interest in rugby at home and I can understand why they don't want to lose that momentum but they also have to consider the welfare of the players."

There is a section of public opinion out there that All Blacks are becoming too mercenary, that they have big bucks in their eyes instead of footballs. It is a glib judgement which takes no account of the players' circumstances on the modern rugby treadmill. I can speak for many players who play the game for the love of it and for the pride they take from being All Blacks but who are finding love and pride increasingly unaffordable. That is a depressing mix of emotions. I think of young comers like Lee Stensness, Marc Ellis, Sam Doyle, Glen Osborne, Carlos Hassan, Simon Mannix (who, I believe, has the goods but was chucked in at the deep end in France), Olo Brown, Laurence Hullena, Mark Allen, Mark Carter, Blair Larsen, Mark Cooksley and the whole legion of players who will become All Blacks and I wonder whether they will be fighting the same wearying Catch-22 battle four years hence.

... "Footballers, it must be remembered, are now just as gentlemanly as they ever were and perfectly entitled to encouragement and kindness. For are they not gratuitous actors and gate-winners...and do they not make personal sacrifices by undertaking their trips in the shape of losing time?" That came from the heart of TR Ellison, captain of New Zealand in 1893, in a little book called The Art of Rugby Football published in 1902. That message is his last word between the covers of a slim document in which he offers "hints and instructions on every point of the game". Mr Ellison's ability to discuss "every point of the game" in a comparative postage-stamp of a book does rather point to the excesses of the law-makers through the years. And his plea for kindly consideration of the players nearly a century ago may just have been the first shot in the long-running battle.

It is the good fortune of New Zealand's young players that they are playing in a country where the administration has become a world leader in getting to terms with the practicalities

– and the humanities – involved in pushing more and more rugby on to the players.

Late last year the International Rugby Board confirmed another five new associate members: Andorra, Chile, Hungary, Luxembourg and Latvia. Yes, Latvia and Andorra. The rugby union game is up and running, no longer the preserve of the tight-knit few who for so many years protected it for themselves. But Bob Dwyer, the Australian coach, has questioned whether even now the IRB understands why it is there. "Contemporary society," he is quoted as saying to English writer David Miller, "respects high-profile professionals more than amateurs, who no longer hold their privileged position...rugby has to protect its ethics, as does

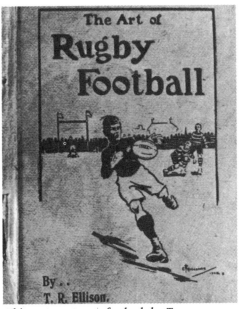

This postage stamp of a book by Tom Ellison, captain of New Zealand in 1893, covered "every point of the game". It was published in 1902.

professional golf, with a rigid moral code. Corruption of the spirit is not a necessary consequence of money. An open structure, as in cricket, is as suitable for rugby. What is needed is an administration that does not stifle development yet maintains the code. That's a difficult role...if the IRB cannot do the job we should find an alternative."

Rugby should long since have shed the miserable philosophy that professionals, or even fringe-professionals, are, therefore, people of inferior degree. I think of Steve Davis, the snooker player, the consummate professional and hardly out of place at an IRB cocktail party, I would have thought. Of Mal Meninga, awesome as a player of rugby league, but the most modest, self-effacing man. Of Allan Border, Australia's cricket captain and a cracker of a decent bloke, but who was messiah one day and pariah the next as the Australian cricket media zoomed in on him during the World Cup matches. Of Richard Hadlee, Susan Devoy, John Wright and Martin Crowe...of all champions professional or amateur because they became what they were through sacrifices and hard work.

The World Cup has had a positive influence on rugby far beyond the boundaries of the participating countries. It has

Bob Dwyer. . ."An open structure, as in cricket, is as suitable for rugby."

heightened awareness of the game everywhere. But it must not detract further from the importance of tours and other test rugby. The World Cup must not become the be-all and end-all of international rugby so that in building toward the next one teams are using test matches experimentally and, therefore, as games of convenience. It would not take long for the public to wake up to that and we would see people staying away from tests just as they have been staying away from club and provincial matches as tests have become normal diet.

Before the opening of the 1992 rugby season a magazine set up the clearly rhetorical question: Whetton and Fox – Why Bother? It did not seek an answer from the two people who were in the best position to provide it. Why bother? I play rugby because I enjoy it. I bother because I enjoy it. Not for the glory, for God's sake. The glory has been. We've been smothered in the glory, five years of it for me, five years which seem to have been filed away under "Forgettable" by some of those who influence public opinion. Had the All Blacks won the World Cup I might well have retired, the last challenge met and fulfilled. So 1991 was a rough year for me and for my family. Bloody rough. But when you go out there on to the field you're on the line, injury or no injury. I did not perform as I, or anyone else, wanted. I did not expect sympathy and I didn't get much. I did not, however, expect the level of abuse and it hurt. If that makes me overly sensitive then that's what I am.

The New Zealand Rugby Union centennial series brought home to me that other than the real battles to be fought on the field against the playing opposition there were the petty, skirmishing actions in which the opposition comprised groups of spectators with closed minds and open mouths, those who, by the simple act of being there, were involved in a great game but who did not deserve any part of it. I refer to them with reluctance and only because their barracking against me became quite a talking point at the time.

It was at an Auckland Rugby Union Christmas party that for the first time after the World Cup I was in the company of many of my friends in rugby. It was a huge enjoyment for me and for my wife. I knew then I did not want to lose this contact.

Why bother to play? Enjoyment was the bottom line, of course, but I played, too, because built into me I had the desire to be the best. Should it have eventuated that I came second, or even third, in that race I could have accepted that, but not if I had defaulted on the challenge. And part of it was all the unanswered ifs. They niggled away at me like an aching tooth. If only I'd been injury-free...if I had been able to give that bit more. I sweated on it all through the summer, undertook the right sort of treatment for the injury and the right sort of training. I decided I did not want to retire on ifs. And I would not be driven out in humiliation as the inflexible has-been some critics, including one who was to become one of the new selection panel, had labelled me. Had I backed out my self-respect would have backed out with me. So I took the risk. New selectors, new coaches, changes of direction. Probably I would need to adjust...and would they want me, anyway? After all the difficulties of 1991 Adele preferred they should not have the chance to drop me. I could understand that. But after years of being in the "certainty" category my motivation was now much as it had been before I became an All Black. The old challenge was now the new.

The centennial series might better have been designated a series of celebration matches than official tests. I see tests as matches between the representatives of two countries and this occasion seemed inappropriate for that status. But coming at a time when New Zealand rugby was under reconstruction the matches were invaluable to the selectors and to the group of outstanding young players who will lead the All Black renaissance. By being selected to play among them I had taken the most important step in the need I felt to re-prove myself – perhaps most importantly, to myself. The elation I felt had little to do with my selection being an answer to anyone. It was the elation and the pride all over again of being an All Black.

Statistics To Dec 31 1991

Compiled by Nick Jordan

HIS CAREER

	M	T	C	PG	DG	TI
Auckland	155	20	505	367	30	2281
New Zealand tests	35	1	103	99	6	525
New Zealand other	27	1	92	48	4	344
NZ Juniors	5	-	13	14	1	71
North Zone	5	-	19	8	-	62
NZ Trials	4	-	7	11	-	47
North Island	3	-	7	5	1	32
NZ Colts	7	1	2	2	2	20
N.I. Universities	1	-	1	4	-	14
Southern Hemisphere	1	-	4	1	-	11
NZ Colts trial	1	-	1	2	-	8
NZ Universities	3	-	-	-	1	3
Barbarians	1	-	-	-	-	-
Totals	248	23	754	561	45	3418

FULL TEST RECORD

1.	v Argentina, Buenos Aires, 1985, 1dg, 3 points.	Won	33-20
2.	v Italy, Auckland 1987, 8c, 2pg, 22.	Won	70-6
3.	v Fiji, Christchurch, 1987, 10c, 2pg, 26.	Won	74-13
4.	v Argentina, Wellington, 1987, 2c, 6pg, 22.	Won	46-15
5.	v Scotland, Christchurch, 1987, 2c, 6pg, 22.	Won	30-3
6.	v Wales, Brisbane, 1987, 7c, 1pg, 17.	Won	49-6
7.	v France, Auckland 1987, 1c, 4pg, 1dg, 17.	Won	29-9
8.	v Australia, Sydney, 1987, 1c, 3pg, 1dg, 14.	Won	30-16
9.	v Wales, Christchurch, 1988, 6c, 12.	Won	52-6
10.	v Wales, Auckland, 1988, 8c, 2pg, 22.	Won	54-9
11.	v Australia, Sydney, 1988, 3c, 2pg, 12.	Won	32-7
12.	v Australia, Brisbane, 1988, 2c, 1pg, 7.	Drew	19-19
13.	v Australia, Sydney, 1988, 3c, 4pg, 18.	Won	30-9
14.	v France, Christchurch, 1989, 2c, 3pg, 13.	Won	25-17
15.	v France, Auckland, 1989, 3c, 4pg, 18.	Won	34-20
16.	v Argentina, Dunedin, 1989, 7c, 2pg, 20.	Won	60-9
17.	v Argentina, Wellington, 1989, 6c, 3pg, 21.	Won	49-12
18.	v Australia, Auckland, 1989, 2c, 4pg, 16.	Won	24-12
19.	v Wales, Cardiff, 1989, 3c, 4pg, 18.	Won	34-9
20.	v Ireland, Dublin, 1989, 1c, 3pg, 11.	Won	23-6
21.	v Scotland, Dunedin, 1990, 1t, 4c, 1pg, 15.	Won	31-16
22.	v Scotland, Auckland, 1990, 1c, 5pg, 17.	Won	21-18
23.	v Australia, Christchurch, 1990, 1c, 1pg, 5.	Won	21-6
24.	v Australia, Auckland, 1990, 3c, 2pg, 1dg, 15.	Won	27-17
25.	v Australia, Wellington, 1990, 2pg, 1dg, 9.	Lost	9-21
26.	v France, Nantes, 1990, 2c, 3pg, 1dg, 16.	Won	24-3
27.	v France, Paris, 1990, 2c, 6pg, 22.	Won	30-12
28.	v Argentina, Buenos Aires, 1991, 1c, 5pg, 17.	Won	28-14
29.	v Argentina, Buenos Aires, 1991, 4c, 4pg, 20.	Won	36-6
30.	v Australia, Sydney, 1991, 1c, 2pg, 8.	Lost	12-21
31.	v Australia, Auckland, 1991, 2pg, 6.	Won	6-3
32.	v England, Twickenham, 1991, 1c, 4pg, 14.	Won	18-12
33.	v Italy, Gloucester, 1991, 3c, 3pg, 15.	Won	31-21
34.	v Canada, Lille, 1991, 3c, 1pg, 9.	Won	29-13
35.	v Australia, Dublin, 1991, 2pg, 6.	Lost	6-16

TEST SUMMARY

	Played	Won	Lost	Drew
v Argentina	6	6	-	-
v Australia	11	7	3	1
v Canada	1	1	-	-
v England	1	1	-	-
v Fiji	1	1	-	-
v France	5	5	-	-
v Ireland	1	1	-	-
v Italy	2	2	-	-
v Scotland	3	3	-	-
v Wales	4	4	-	-
Total	35	31	3	1

RECORDS HELD

For Auckland

		Previous holder		When Broken
Most points	2281	S.L. Watt	419	v Waikato 25/8/84
Most matches by back	155	M.A. Herewini	139	v Southland 8/9/90
Most conv match	12			
(equal with B.M. Craies)		9 by three players		
Most conv season	77 (1990)	R.R. Dunn	23	Eq 1982. Br 1984, 90.
Most pen match	7	6 by two players		
Most pen season	48 (1989, 1990)	S.L. Watt	28	Br 1984, 89. Eq 1990.
Most dg season	8 (1990)	5 by two players		Eq 1987. Br 1990.
Most points match	31	25 M.C.M. Cormack		v Marlb 25/9/84
Most points season	322 (1990)	R.R. Dunn	142	Br 1983, 84, 89, 90.

For NZ tests

		Previous holder		When broken	
Most points	525	D.B. Clarke	207	v Australia	30/7/88
Most conv	103	D.B. Clarke	33	v Wales	25/5/88
Most pen	99	A.R. Hewson	43	v Argentina	29/7/89
Most dg	6	D.B. Clarke/M.A. Herewini	5	v France	3/11/90
Most capped 1st five	35	W.R. Smith	17	v Australia	5/8/89
Most points match	26	equal with A.R. Hewson		v Fiji	27/5/87
Most conv match	10	A.R. Hewson	6	v Italy	22/5/87 (8)
				then v Fiji	27/5/87 (10)
Most pen match	6	equal with D.B. Clarke/K.J. Crowley		v Argentina	1/6/87
				v Scotland	6/6/87
				v France	10/11/90

For NZ all matches

		Previous holder		When broken	
Most points	869	D.B. Clarke	781	v Argentina	6/7/91
Most conversions	195	D.B. Clarke	173	v France	10/11/90
Most pen	147	D.B. Clarke	120	v Tucuman	25/6/91
Most conv match	15	equal with J.F. Karam		v Japan	1/11/87

First class		Previous holder		When broken	
Most points	3418	W.F. McCormick	2065	Akl v Otago	24/9/88
Most conv	754	W.F. McCormick	487	Akl v Fiji	7/5/89
Most pen	561	D.B. Clarke	320	Akl v Manawatu	17/9/88
Most points any province	2281	W.F. McCormick (Canty)	1297	Akl v Taranaki	13/8/88
Most points in season (1981)	433	R.M. Deans	281	1984, 1987, 1989	
Most conv season(1989)	103	R.M. Deans	53	1984, 1987, 1989	
Most pen season (1989)	72	R.M. Deans	45	Eq 1984. Br 1987, 1989.	

Ranfurly Shield		Previous holder		When broken	
Most points	748	R.M. Deans	339	v Hawkes Bay	31/8/88
Most conv	187	R.M. Deans	62	v Counties	3/10/87
Most pen	113	R.M. Deans	57	v Manawatu	17/9/88
Most conv match	12	equal B.M. Craies		v Nelson Bays	13/4/91
Most pen match	7	equal R.M. Deans		v Canterbury	6/10/90

MISCELLANEOUS

Test

Average:	15 points
Wins:	91%
0-9 points:	23%
10-19:	51%
20+:	26%
v Agentina:	103pts in 6
v Australia:	116 in 11
v Canada:	9 in 1
v England:	14 in 1
v Fiji:	26 in 1
v France:	86 in 5
v Ireland:	11 in 1
v Italy:	37 in 2
v Scotland:	54 in 3
v Wales:	69 in 4

Auckland

Average:	14.72	
Ranfurly Shield:	748pts in 44	(17.00 ave)
National Champ:	1291 in 91	(14.18)
Wins:	92%	
0-9 points:	19%	
10-20%:	61%	
20+:	20%	

All First Class

Average:	13.78	
Wins:	92%	
0-9pts:	25%	
10-19:	56%	
20+:	19%	
in NZ:	2644 in 187	(14.14)
Overseas:	774 in 61	(12.69)
On Eden Park:	1331 in 83	(16.03)